Born in Soweto

Born in Soweto

Inside the Heart of South Africa

Heidi Holland

PENGUIN BOOKS

PENGUIN BOOKS

Published by the Penguin Group
27 Wrights Lane, London W8 5TZ, England
Viking Penguin, a division of Penguin Books USA Inc, 375 Hudson Street, New York, New York 10014, USA
Penguin Books Australia Ltd, Ringwood, Victoria, Australia
Penguin Books Canada Ltd, 10 Alcorn Avenue, Toronto, Ontario, Canada M4V 3B2
Penguin Books (NZ) Ltd, 182-190 Wairau Road, Auckland 10, New Zealand
Penguin Books, Amethyst Street, Theta Ext 1, Johannesburg, South Africa

Penguin Books Ltd, Registered Offices: Harmondsworth, Middlesex, England

First published by Penguin Books 1994

Copyright © Heidi Holland 1994

ISBN 0 140 24446 8

Typeset by Iskova Image Setting
Printed and bound by Creda Press
Cover design by Graphicor

Front cover illustration by Tommy Motswai
Lenyalo at home from Rockville, 1988
Courtesy of Mrs L Givon

For
DUNCAN

CONTENTS

ACKNOWLEDGEMENTS

Writing this book has been more of a revelation than simply a journalistic venture. It has taken me into the lives of great, unsung South Africans, whose remarkable achievements in adversity give humbling insights into the pain and resilience that is etched deep in the hearts of the people of Soweto. I thank the many Sowetans who generously gave time, trust and their stories, which will resonate within me for ever.

Sowetans Jimmy Ntintili, tour operator, and Victor Matom, photographer, kindly accompanied me into Soweto on several occasions when I thought it too risky to go alone. Both contributed to the book in other ways — Victor with his telling photographs and Jimmy as an endless source of information.

Authors Martin Meredith and Jenny Hobbs scrutinised the first draft and introduced some important changes. Yusuf and Amina Cachalia, distinguished political activists, gave me wise advice. Educationalist Michael Rice, encouraging from the start, kept a keen eye on syntax. My editors at Penguin, Alison Lowry and Pam Thornley, contributed their invaluable experience.

My parents, Les and Idely Holland, and my sons, Jonah and Niko, were as always patiently supportive. Journalist Nonie Niesewand and photographer Louise Gubb, my talented soul-sisters, gave me ideas and terrific encouragement during a difficult year.

Chaologist Duncan Clarke, my friend for many years, believes passionately in this book. His vision is its most inspiring influence beyond the Sowetans themselves.

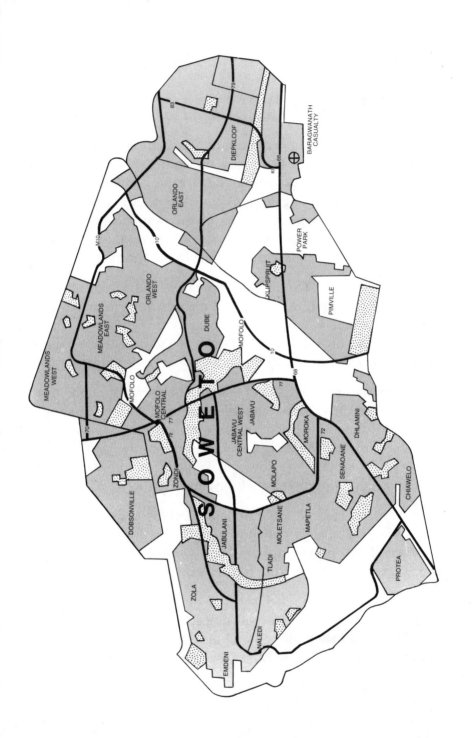

PREFACE

*Readers who are familiar with the South African
politics that gave rise to townships like Soweto
may prefer to page past this first section,
intended for those who have little
background knowledge.*

S oweto is a vast, impoverished and violent city that
epitomises downtrodden black South Africa. No other
name, apart from that of Nelson Mandela, evokes the images of
black defiance of white rule that spring to mind at the mention
of Soweto.

Though typical of black South Africa's living conditions,
Soweto is also unique, a phenomenon in its own right. Today
the most violent city in the world, Soweto is the result of
urbanisation perverted by apartheid. It is a forsaken and hostile
place, even to most of the four million people who call it
home.

Although Soweto is known internationally as a city,
Sowetans refer to it as a township. Lacking most signs of a
modern metropolis, it is actually a mass fusion of thirty-three
townships, which were called 'locations' in apartheid
terminology. Some of these component slums have names
that are widely recognised, such as Kliptown and Meadowlands. It was in Kliptown in 1955 that the country's largest
political movement, the African National Congress (ANC),
adopted its Freedom Charter — the programme of the South
African liberation struggle. Meadowlands is where the

dispossessed black residents of Sophiatown — a lively, free-thinking township that was literally bulldozed out of existence by the Pretoria government in the 1950s — were resettled.

Meadowlands' fame during the 1980s and 1990s is the result of constant television and newspaper coverage of violence that flares there relentlessly, between political rivals and domestic enemies alike.

Today sprawling across fifty square miles, Soweto began to grow in the south western area of Johannesburg during the early 1950s: its name is an acronym for South Western Townships. Several slums, like Pimville and Orlando, were already there. The site was chosen because it was bounded by industrial districts where many of Soweto's inhabitants worked, and because it was separated from white areas by open land that could easily be controlled and defended by security forces in the event of trouble.

Soweto was deliberately situated far away from Johannesburg's city centre because whites did not want to encounter the hovels and destitution which characterised the lot of most urban blacks, who had to commute twenty miles or more to work each morning. For many years the government resisted pressure to connect Soweto with the main highway now linking it to Johannesburg, not only because the state's security advisers wanted to be able to seal Soweto off in the event of revolt, but also on the grounds that such a connection might result in white travellers from outside Johannesburg accidentally driving into Soweto. White South Africans were not only indifferent to the welfare of urban blacks: they were also scared of them.

Like all recently urbanised people, Sowetans are a transitional species caught between two cultures — traditional African and modern European. They have changed their lifestyle more in the last seventy years than in the previous two hundred. It has been an especially painful process in South Africa because whites, observing that blacks living in towns created hygienic, economic and social problems for which the state was unwilling to find solutions, regarded blacks in the cities as a disagreeable and disposable temporary labour force.

When Africans first came in large numbers to the booming gold mining mecca of Johannesburg in the 1920s, government policy decreed they should be allowed to enter the city only in order to work for whites, and they must depart for the rural areas when such work was completed. For generations preceding Afrikaner rule, it was uncritically assumed that the black population could be auxiliary to white enterprise and yet continue living within the rural system.

Successive white governments tried very hard to prevent blacks from establishing city roots. The rise of an aggressive Afrikaner nationalism with its apartheid doctrine, developed during the 1950s, inspired a number of laws specifically aimed at turning blacks into homeless, familyless migrants.

In the years before Afrikaner rule, the campaign against black urban settlement changed dramatically with the outbreak of World War Two in 1939, when influx control was temporarily suspended in order to recruit labour for rapidly expanding factories producing war materials. By 1946 Johannesburg's white residents had increased by 29 per cent while the city's black population had grown by nearly 70 per cent to an estimated 400 000. Restrictions were subsequently reintroduced but by then the government had lost the battle: blacks had come to South Africa's cities to stay.

For over forty years thereafter, it was government policy to make the townships unappealing in the hope that blacks would not be tempted to settle in them. The establishment of old age homes, orphanages and other charities was actively discouraged. Informal private sector enterprise was penalised because it offered prosperity to township blacks, and because white businessmen wanted Sowetans to buy exclusively from white-owned shops.

Foremost among apartheid architect Hendrik Verwoerd's influx control rules were the hated pass laws, which rendered black people permanently insecure in the cities because they were entitled to live there only if employed, a status that could be rescinded at any time. Those women and children who managed to slip past the authorities and live in Soweto illegally knew that the family was always threatened by the eviction of one or all of its members, that administrative pressure would relentlessly bear upon it. 'The necessity for some form of influx control may be debatable,' wrote a sociologist in the 1940s. 'But there cannot be any debate about the gross injustice of denying a man who is legally qualified to be in Johannesburg the right to have his wife join him. A country that does this gives the lie to its professed concern for the sanctity of family life.'

One of Verwoerd's laws denied widows the right to rent homes. 'Some officials demand that the widow must come to their offices a day after the funeral of her husband to discuss the question of the house,' reported a bereaved woman. Even if a widow managed to get a pass from a lenient official, her children and other dependants were frequently sent back to a rural village.

Soweto's population totalled 1.4 million in the early 1970s. The chronic shortage of housing that characterised the three previous decades remained unalleviated, becoming more demoralising with each successive year. Today's Sowetans who are lucky enough to live in houses rather than in makeshift shacks still pack themselves tightly into small rooms, often sharing ten square metres of floor space with five or six others at night.

In 1958, British writer James Morris recorded the following description of the township: 'As far as I could see, stretching interminably away into the dusk, the houses of the township lay there blankly. A few candles flickered here and there... it is the deliberate impersonality of the locations that is most terrible... you cannot escape the suspicion that this severe barracks-like order is intended to subjugate the African, to impress upon him his inferior status, to prove that he is not in white South Africa by right, but only on sufferance.' Very little has changed in the intervening years.

The state's educational structures for black children were distinctly inferior to those provided in the white community. Blacks were to be educated sufficiently to serve their white masters, but no further. Thus life in Soweto was at all times anchored to the political system that fashioned it. Inadequate housing, insanitary conditions, crowded and ill-equipped schools, lack of jobs, lack of social services and recreational facilities — added to the humiliation of being a black person in a disdainful white world — were the circumstances in which generations of Sowetans grew up.

Ordinary Sowetans were assailed not only by white South Africa's politics but by increasing pressure from black politicians exhorting them to participate in the turmoil of the liberation struggle. During the 1970s, revolutionary power rose up as never before to challenge, and in many cases confound, the black man in the street.

The long-established African National Congress, and in later years the Pan-Africanist Congress (PAC) — both banned in 1960 — had been trying since the early years of the century to redress black grievances. Although the ANC had established a loyal if largely inactive mass following among South African blacks, it had not succeeded in bringing about the mental revolution required to confront apartheid effectively.

A dynamic force that burst into Sowetan homes during the 1970s, a philosophy known as Black Consciousness, successfully mobilised black resistance to apartheid. It was based on the premise that oppression was essentially a psychological problem. The new movement's charismatic leader, a young medical student named Steve Biko, believed blacks needed to shake off the inferiority complex bequeathed to them by generations of white masters demanding subservience. Biko achieved a new mood of militant pride among urban blacks.

Within a few years Black Consciousness was sweeping university campuses throughout the country. Achieving an unprecedented level of political education, it spread beyond the universities into thousands of schools, especially those in Soweto.

During the early hours of 16 June 1976, thousands of schoolchildren marched in Soweto in protest against a government instruction that Afrikaans had to be used as one of the media of tuition in secondary schools. They were fired on by police. One child was killed and several injured. Enraged by the use of force to smash a peaceful protest, the students went on the rampage. Bricks, stones and bottles flew through the air. Soldiers in helicopters dropped rifles and ammunition. Shots rang out and more students fell. Wounded teenagers lay bleeding among their classmates; hysterical screams pierced the roar of indignation and stampeding feet. But the angry crowd kept advancing towards the police, hurling abuse and missiles at them. Alarmed white officers retreated to await reinforcements, by which time the students were setting cars and buildings alight.

Nothing could quell the anger. By midday on 16 June the sky over Soweto was filled with dark clouds of smoke and dust. Fifteen people died in the township that day. By the end of the first week of the uprising, one hundred and fifty lives had been lost in Soweto alone. By October the following year, seven hundred people had died in countrywide anti-apartheid protests. Over 90 per cent of the dead were less than twenty-three years old.

The death of so many young people was a terrible price to pay but South Africa's youth had scored significant political victories. The protest sparked off repeated boycotts of classes throughout the country: five hundred secondary school teachers in Soweto resigned their posts, signalling not only the collapse of high school education in the township but the unprecedented power of the students. Another campaign led by the students against proposed rent increases in Soweto was so successful that it resulted in the collapse of the government-appointed civic administration and the establishment in its place of the most democratic local authority ever seen in the township, the Committee of Ten. Furthermore, the courage displayed by the students in confronting white authority on 16 June 1976 inspired thousands of formerly submissive adults to join the ensuing protests.

The consequences of the students' uprising were to affect the lives of Sowetans for many years to come. The rebellion succeeded in achieving political solidarity across the generation gap previously dividing conservative older blacks from their militant children. This was a major political advantage enabling revolutionary organisations like the banned African National Congress to mobilise the black masses against the government in later years.

Another outcome of the students' revolt was its long-term effect on parental authority. Part of the impetus for the uprising had come from the students' rejection of their parents' authority: Black Consciousness had taught the youth to examine critically all the forces that enabled whites to keep blacks subjugated, and the students concluded that their parents' generation was culpable by default.

Believing, for example, that their parents had been lulled into political passivity in the numerous beer-halls provided by Soweto's white-run municipality, the students had singled out these drinking establishments as arson targets: sixty-seven of them had been burnt to the ground by the end of June 1976. 'It is our parents who have let things go on far too long without doing anything. They have failed,' was a typical comment from one of the marching students to a reporter in 1976. Not only did they lose respect for the older generation at a political level, but thousands of students throughout Soweto rejected their parents' values in a much wider context. In a society which traditionally venerated age as the source of communal authority, many parents were no longer able to control or even influence the behaviour of their children.

Thousands of teenagers, whether fleeing arrest by the South African police or determined to take up arms against their white oppressors, left the country after 1976 to enlist in the ANC's military wing. Younger siblings at home in Soweto, mesmerised by the heroism of older brothers and sisters who espoused a new culture of defiance and violence, found those basically antisocial values more important than society's.

In the old days of family unity, all the adults involved in a child's upbringing told the child what was right and wrong. Now the parents, accepting with shame that it had been left to their teenagers to score crucial victories for the revolutionary cause but distrusting the means by which that end had been achieved, were no longer sure which values they ought to impart. Many mothers and fathers admitted to being frightened of their militant children, as were schoolteachers.

It was a confusion in which few definite moral guidelines could be enshrined by the family, society's traditional custodian of healthy values. It was to lead to a crime wave of unprecedented proportions; a disrespect for human life that was to make murder almost endemic in Soweto in later years.

Another blow dealt to the long-term stability of life in Soweto was the habitual boycotting of schools which followed the political successes of the 1976 students' revolt. During the 1980s, the exiled ANC and its internal protest movements urged schoolchildren to vacate their desks and reject the inferior education offered by the oppressor. 'Liberation Before Education' was the slogan chanted by hundreds of thousands of children for over a decade. Scorning the warnings of parents who knew from bitter experience how few opportunities were open in a modern economy for people with scant education, a new generation of Sowetans followed the example of the students of 1976 and sacrificed their educations in the interests of the struggle.

By 1990, having realised how damaging a policy school boycotts would prove in years to come, the ANC urged children to return to their classrooms. But by then the damage was done. The majority of the children who should have achieved at least a basic education during the previous fourteen years were without qualifications. Some were illiterate. They had advanced the struggle but in so doing had been left without a viable stake in the future. Described as 'the lost generation' even by the ANC, or as 'cannon fodder' by more cynical observers, these young men and women were to grow increasingly embittered as they realised that their sacrifice had left them severely handicapped economically.

Poverty has always been the mainspring of Soweto's acute and painful problems. In the mid-1980s, economic conditions deteriorated more rapidly than in the past. With a campaign of countrywide boycotts of schools, white-owned businesses, rent payments and government transport — orchestrated by the ANC's organisations operating legally inside South Africa — came increasing violence between activists and security forces, and a spate of repressive laws. The international community responded by launching a barrage of economic sanctions aimed at forcing a change in government policy. Causing severe losses to industry and commerce, on top of the chaos in the work-force resulting from labour stayaways and sustained violence in the townships, sanctions steadily eroded employment opportunities for blacks. By the 1990s, up to 60 per cent of Soweto's adults were unemployed.

Crime became the most common way for the jobless to get cash. In a desperate situation of entrenched poverty, lack of skills, illiteracy and homelessness, some scavenged, sold drugs or scrap, and gambled; others took in washing and ironing or turned to prostitution and begging. But by far the most popular means of survival was stealing.

The escalating crime wave was not confined to the young. Many parents also became unwilling criminals in order to pay school fees and feed their families. Theft became an increasingly accepted norm in Soweto as the community censure which had controlled it in earlier years fell away. Young children saw adult thieves as role models. A moral distinction emerged between the habitual criminal who stole, raped and killed on a regular basis and the serial thief who felt justified in stealing, often with the aid of violence, because he desperately needed money. An expensively dressed 22-year-old, describing in detail how he and two friends periodically go to Johannesburg in search of a car to steal, looked hurt when referred to in the interview as a thief. 'Don't call me that,' he pleaded.

In the 1990s, crime has become an inescapable part of urban life in South Africa. The contrast between the conspicuous affluence of white suburbs and the squalor of Soweto has made white householders the most legitimate targets. But in the face of the hard economic realities of endemic unemployment, everyone who is better off becomes a victim, to the extent that residents in the poorer parts of Soweto are unable to leave clothes on a washline unattended.

The hardest hit in the vicious crime wave engulfing Johannesburg are Sowetans themselves, not whites. Whites have resorted to elaborate security measures including killer dogs and electrified fences. But Soweto remains the country's crime hot-spot: illegal acts committed there are more violent than anywhere else in South Africa.

Soweto's crime rate is twice that of New York City. The township's Flying Squad receives four hundred and fifty emergency calls a week. Four corpses are discovered every weekday in Soweto's dusty streets; more over weekends. Many of the victims have been brutally murdered for the sake of the miserable sums of money they were carrying. Over three hundred unnatural deaths are investigated every month.

The lives of a large number of young Sowetans have been rooted in political violence since their schooldays. Having no jobs and nothing rewarding to do with their time for unending months and years, many of these young people call themselves comrades of the struggle for political liberation but unleash their anger and frustration on their own people. It is commonplace in Soweto for gunmen to enter houses and fire randomly at families sitting at home watching television. Such violence usually flares after political rallies or funerals of residents murdered by unknown assailants. In a ruthless cycle of killing and revenge, no one is safe in Soweto at night.

The housing shortage in the township is so acute — particularly since influx control was abolished in the reforms introduced during the early years of the 1990s — that thousands of people living in backyard shacks and squatter settlements are abandoned to the terrors of the night, having no locking doors in their tumbledown homes. Many of the young victims of sexual abuse, which has reached epidemic proportions in Soweto, are raped while sleeping in their own beds. Overcrowding breeds terrible crimes, even within families. It is not unusual for twenty people to be sharing a forty square metre, four-roomed house. Most of the child victims of sexual abuse live in such conditions.

The urban black family, always insecure, is today beset by chronic instability and conflict. The loss of traditional ways, coupled with humiliating difficulties experienced in adapting to Western forms of behaviour, have left the older generation with a sense of hopelessness that all too often finds relief in alcoholism. Younger people seek outlets for their frustration in the shadowy underworld of crime and social vengeance that often poses as popular justice.

Nothing illustrates the moral confusion and deep-rooted brutality of Soweto more sombrely than the local justice dispensed in 'people's courts' that have been operating since violence became a way of life during the 1980s. At one such hearing of one hundred and fifty accusers judging two 13-year-olds suspected of theft, a middle-aged man called for the death penalty. Another demanded that the boys' fingers be chopped off. The two accused sat huddled together on the floor, shaking in terror, their faces and limbs swollen and bleeding after repeated assaults. Someone called for their eyes to be gouged out with a screwdriver. Another man suggested their kneecaps be smashed. Just as a vote was passed to kill the boys, a civic authority arrived and pleaded for conventional justice. Howls of protest drowned his words. Finally, he demanded the names of those who wanted to execute the children. No one stepped forward, and the people's court reluctantly agreed that the accused be handed over to the police.

During the 1990s, when South Africa's white government realised it had no option but to negotiate a power transfer with blacks, Soweto became one of the battlegrounds of rivalry between the popular African National Congress and the minority, Zulu-dominated Inkatha Freedom Party. While the country's future was at last under discussion at the negotiating table, groups lacking numerical supremacy sought to maximise their strength through brutality. Reports of bizarre massacres on Soweto's trains and in its communities became common-place. No one admitted culpability. Black political foes accused each other — and the police. Innocent people died every day in some of the bloodiest killings in South Africa's history. Evidence uncovered shortly before the country's first demo-cratic election in 1994 implicated high-ranking policemen in the hit squad activity that had been tearing apart townships like Soweto since late 1989.

Many people in Soweto have had their kind instincts eroded by hardship and pain. They have lost a way of looking with pleasure at the rising and setting sun; of upholding the ideals of liberty which they have sought for so long; of caring for one another. Materialism, in the form of white greed and black poverty, has exacted an intolerably high price. Political emancipation has often served as a justification for far less noble deeds than the leaders of the struggle would ever publicly commend.

Many, many more Sowetans are peaceful men and women who simply want to lead ordinary lives. But even so modest a goal is hard to achieve in Soweto today. The old way — in which the family was the focal point of all its members and all contributed to its welfare — has gone. A large proportion of Soweto's children grow up in single parent families with the mother working by day and moonlighting for extra money at night. The women, especially, make a valiant effort to raise healthy children amid turmoil and poverty. Their contribution is generally undervalued, their potential untapped in a patriarchal society. Because of the economic need for mothers to work in the city for long hours and the lack of facilities to take care of children in their absence, the very young are often neglected. It is not unusual in Soweto's clinics to see a five-year-old child clutching a desperately ill baby sibling, waiting patiently in a queue for medical help.

Virtually all Sowetans have experienced formidable adversity. Most manage to keep humour in their minds and hope in their hearts. Theirs is a timeless struggle to survive against impossible odds. Though some suffering has been alleviated by the political reforms of the 1990s, poverty and violence remain to challenge the ingenuity and resources of South Africa's rulers for a long time to come.

Much has been said over the years about the Sowetans' collective resistance to oppression. Little has been written about their individual lives. This book seeks to redress the gap in the literature of Soweto. Not even history at its most reckless should rob people of the right to their own stories.

1

Dawn

In the hour before dawn, a pall of coal smoke hangs like a grubby shroud over Soweto, blotting out stars and obscuring the moon. A steady stream of shadowy figures, including children, elderly people and others in the prime of life, sets out on the road to Maraisburg, a town on the western outskirts of Johannesburg where the city's central garbage dump is situated. An hour's walk from Soweto, it is a popular place to scavenge for food and saleable goods amid refuse discarded by the white inhabitants of Johannesburg.

The houses of the township line its streets in tightly packed rows of monotonous uniformity. But they are not as regimented as they appear to be. Small opportunities for originality have been explored in the wrought-iron burglar proofing added to windows and doors, some featuring baroque winged angels blowing trumpets or flowers and animal heads twisted together. Doors have been painted in hot colours. Plants in plastic flower pots and jam tins adorn some entrances; cactuses protrude from dusty rockeries. Most of the windows display lace curtains of varied design.

Few cars are parked outside but it is not unusual to see a dilapidated vehicle near a smart one because, in Soweto, a successful businessman often lives next door to a humble trader, or a beggar. Distinctions in social status were not deemed necessary by the white men who planned Soweto. The township was not designed as a residential area for people with different temperaments and preferences. It was merely a reservoir of labour in which expressions of individuality were discouraged.

The residents of Soweto range from washerwomen to models, artisans to artists. Homes in a particularly impoverished area like Chiawelo, furnished with little more than grass sleeping mats and a few cooking utensils, are occupied by men, women and children with nothing to do all day. Those who work — around 40 per cent of the adult population of Soweto — spend most of their time outside the home inhabiting a world in Johannesburg where their unemployed relatives are aliens. In Dube, owner-built homes represent the Mayfair of Soweto: they are occupied by people who would be middle-class in any society. But they are a tiny minority: the vast majority of Sowetans confront poverty and destitution from the day they are born until the day they die.

There is much evidence in Soweto of the range of trouble suffered by residents. The remains of a burnt-out school stand on a street corner, a relic of the flame of revolt that was lit during the students' uprising in 1976. Nearby is a ruined block of government administration offices, gutted by revolutionary hands that hurled rocks eighteen years ago but later held submachine guns and grenades. An occupied hostel, with almost every pane of glass smashed, evokes numbing images of the bloody wars that have been fought in these and similar precincts by rival political groups in recent years. The charred brick shell of a house, minus roof, doors and windows, bears testimony to a revenge attack against a suspected police informer. Squatters have taken up residence here, though it offers little protection against the icy winds of winter.

Having a house to live in, whatever its condition, is considered a luxury by most Sowetans. The township's squatter camps symbolise the plight of the homeless. In the pre-dawn gloom, these settlements are a jumbled mess of corrugated iron, packing crates and cardboard boxes, un-hinged doors wedged at impossible angles, bits of timber, and canvas flapping in the wind. Thousands of people are sleeping in a scrapyard known as Mandela Village in Diepkloof, though the flickering light of a single candle and the crying of a baby are the only signs of life.

The housing backlog in Soweto is estimated at 100 000 units. Although the shortage has become more acute since the removal of influx controls in the apartheid reforms of the 1990s, there has never been sufficient accommodation for the township's residents. Soweto was created by the government to ensure that the blacks who were needed as workers in Johannesburg's white-owned factories and businesses did not live in or near white residential areas. Men-only hostels, rather than houses, were built to accommodate workers during the early years of Soweto's history: married contract workers were expected to stay in the city without their wives and families.

The odd car moves through the mist and smoke; a dog barks in the distance. Driving westwards through Orlando, one of the oldest areas of Soweto, you pass few shops. There are only a handful of business centres in the entire township, a legacy of white commercial greed. Determined to ensure that Sowetans spent their money in white-owned businesses in Johannesburg, the government effectively prohibited industrial and commer-cial development in the township. Blacks could in theory get permission from local state administrators to open shops or businesses but such requests were invariably denied. Instead, black entrepreneurial initiatives were driven underground, often into crime but also into backyard shops called spazas, a word meaning 'hidden' in township slang. Stocking basic commodities like bread, soft drinks, detergents and cooking ingredients, spazas remained undetected by the authorities for many years.

Among Soweto's few conventional business developments is a complex in Mofolo of shops, offices and a rare cinema. The owner is Ephraim Tshabalala, who became mayor of Soweto in 1983 and swiftly set about feathering his own nest with township funds. Hated by Sowetans for collaborating with white authorities and exploiting the poor, Tshabalala's buildings have been attacked and rebuilt many times over the years. The people of Soweto charge Tshabalala with many betrayals, not least his statement in 1965 that 'apartheid is a blessing for Africans'. Rude graffiti and political slogans, shrieking abuse in the moonlight, are scrawled on his walls. He paints over the angry words but they reappear, again and again.

Tempers are short in Soweto, and bad memories haunt every street. 'Life owes you nothing. You owe everything to Life', declares a message on a wall. Not long ago, a passing American news photographer found a dead man lying beneath this slogan. Like so many hapless victims in crime-ridden Soweto, he had been stabbed by unknown assailants.

At 5.30 a.m. lights begin to shine in bedroom windows and wisps of smoke trail from coal stoves that have been lit for breakfast. The smell of sulphur dioxide intensifies. Birds offer greetings to a new day; the distant crow of a cockerel sets off a cacophony of shrill answers. Open fires are burning in a stretch of veld and huddled men in balaclavas lean over the flames, warming their hands.

In a main road near Baragwanath, the largest hospital in Africa, Soweto's central taxi rank is already busy. Three bright braziers burn hectically on the roadside, in preparation for peanut vendors and those who will come to roast mealie cobs. Women wrapped in blankets emerge from behind a rural bus, dazzled by the approaching headlamps and staggering under the weight of suitcases balanced on their heads. One carries a cooking pot and a suitcase as she struggles to hoist her baby on to her back. Taxis are converging quickly, loading passengers and driving away, bumper to bumper as far as the eye can see through the smoke and ever-whirling dust.

By 5.45 a.m., away from the main thoroughfare, there is a steady murmur, like waves on a distant shore: the sound of thousands of workers arising from sleep, grumbling, yawning, stretching cramped arms and legs, shivering in the cold morning.

A police station, with a banner announcing the opening of Sof Town Jazz Club hanging from its barbed wire fence, is well lit, busy processing the dockets of crimes committed during the night. Humble hessian-covered stalls stand empty on the roadside, waiting to be stocked for the day by traders selling fruit, vegetables and cigarettes: recent reforms have legalised such businesses. People are spilling into the streets in large numbers now; the old walking stiffly while young men run for warmth. Sparrows chatter in a tree bearing stillborn plums. The moon, now pale, is still in the sky.

Passengers queue at the station near Jabulani. The first of many train massacres, an extraordinary horror peculiar to South Africa, occurred here a few years ago. Dark figures appear around a street corner, perhaps residents of the nearby hostel from where the train killers came. The hostel's rows of dormitories stretch far back, their broken windows a sign of the turbulent times, the restraining fence a recent addition.

The hostels are remnants of rural South Africa transplanted into the city. Most of their occupants are contract workers who originally came to town on a temporary basis. They have left their families — and often their hearts — in faraway villages.

'Beaut by Dr Fingertips' reads a sign over a derelict hut. The burnt-out shell of a house looms ahead. Daylight reveals the backyards of houses, many of them crammed with corrugated iron shacks where tenants live. A police armoured vehicle rumbles along the distant highway. A train jam-packed with humanity chugs by, half-seen through the haze. Those who cannot afford the fare stand on narrow running boards, their bodies pressed against steel carriages. Stories of numerous freeloaders who have slipped on to the tracks and suffered terrifying deaths or injuries abound in Soweto. In recent times, commuters have been terrorised by sinister train killings committed by hooded murderers wielding pangas, axes and guns for undeclared political motives.

Litter is banked up against the walls and fences, swept there by the fierce winds of August. Plastic bags hang from the branches of leafless trees. 'The New Jesus Exhaust Team' proclaims its same-day service from a placard wired to a lamp-post. The moon, almost transparent, is sinking. A junior football team practises in a dirt patch. Fires burn on the touchline and gusts of wind swirl smoke, dust and ash about.

A line of packed taxis passes in a rush. Stickers on misted windows proclaim SABTA, the South African Black Taxi Association, an institution that has played a central role in the burgeoning black economic revolution being waged alongside the political struggle for equality. With over 60 000 member-operators of minibuses, SABTA has fostered the entrepreneurial spirit among tens of thousands of blacks who have seen it grow from a small fleet to a successful rival of the government's rudimentary train and bus services. SABTA's operation has improved the lives of millions of workers in recent years: instead of rising from their beds in the pre-dawn hours to walk to far-flung stations and bus stops, Sowetans now hail minibuses that collect passengers in every street.

A wheelbarrow stacked high with beer crates inches its way into the yard of a house that looks like an ordinary home but is actually a shebeen, a drinking establishment. Sowetans drink more beer than any other urban group in the world. Shebeens date back to the days when the selling of alcohol to blacks was forbidden; the days of regular police liquor raids when the charismatic widows who sold booze illegally from their homes became known as shebeen queens.

It is 6.00 a.m. and a group of children clutching cases and books are hurrying to school. Some walk for many miles because their parents cannot afford taxi fares. They leap over a pool of stagnant water; a small girl jumps short and starts to cry. 'Car Wash' is painted on a tin lid tied to a stick nearby. This is the place in Dobsonville where three men were brutally murdered a few nights ago. Neighbours said 'people from nowhere' came to kill them.

A well-dressed man is coming up a river bank, picking his way carefully through piles of litter. Bits of shattered glass shine like dew in the dust. The distant rumble of a train is blurred by the clatter of people running to catch taxis. 'Viva ANC' declares a slogan painted over a window of planks of wood instead of glass. Two coal-delivery ponies chomp hungrily, their heads buried in a massive bucket, a heavy trailer hitched behind them. 'Long Live the People's Army', says a sign.

Zola, a particularly violent area in Soweto, stretches out in straight lines. Patients are already queuing outside its clinic. Jabulani Stadium, where many political rallies have been held over the years, is deserted but for a child who stands shivering at the entrance, clutching an orange and looking anxiously down the street. Taxis are queuing at a petrol station, their radios blaring from different channels.

The steps of Regina Mundi Church, a famous Sowetan political landmark which contains the country's only black Madonna, are being swept by an energetic woman. Several scruffy black ducks and a dog scavenge in a rubbish dump.

Kliptown Station is crowded. A man in an overcoat dances in the street ahead, his arms held high in the air. Two small schoolboys deep in conversation bump into him and hesitate for a long time, looking confused. The roofs of some of the more dilapidated houses near the station are held down by large boulders to prevent their being carried away by the wind. A tiny child staggers home with a sack of oranges on his back. Men and women carrying large boxes packed with bread are making their way to Chicken Farm, a squatter settlement lying in a shallow valley beside the road, a blanket of smoke and mist hiding its sad shapes. Armoured vehicles cruise by.

* * *

In the Pimville area of Soweto is a yellow facebrick house with no distinguishing features. Set in a street with no name alongside many identical dwellings, it is unlit and bare in the breaking light. There was once an attempt to establish a garden but no plants survive in the bed of trampled weeds. A mound of refuse lies beside a broken gate that has been hitched crookedly to its post.

This is the home of 78-year-old George Resenga and his family of sixteen people. There are eleven grandchildren, two daughters, a son and a daughter-in-law sleeping in the four-roomed house. They are among the poorest residents of Soweto. Nobody in the family has a job: they all survive on

George's pension of 275 rands (50 pounds) a month. The old man has never met any of the fathers of his grandchildren: all were born out of wedlock, mostly at a time when their mothers were barely more than children themselves.

Six of the other children are asleep on the living-room-cum-kitchen floor. The furniture — two sagging sofas and a chair — has been piled in a corner. There are no ceiling boards; the asbestos roof is black from coal smoke. The temperature in the room is below freezing.

Two boys are lying close together on a blanket spread under the kitchen table. Their bodies are completely concealed by a second blanket tucked over their heads. Two other forms lie opposite, similarly covered, with one protruding foot wearing a shoe full of holes. A few school garments are stretched over the chair to prevent creasing. A third mound of blanket is in the corner beside the front door; two young girls are asleep beneath it.

Everyone in Soweto fears the invasion of dangerous forces — human, reptilian and spiritual — during the night, says George's daughter, Linda. They would rather sleep on the floor than on the sofas, she says, because snakes, spiders and evil spirits can hide under furniture, whereas nothing can crawl under a blanket that is tightly wedged beneath the body. The boys lying under the kitchen table have rehearsed a defence strategy in the event of human invasion, she explains. They will rise up together and, with arms outstretched, heave the table in the faces of intruders approaching through the front door.

The other members of the family are asleep on the floors of two tiny bedrooms. A red plastic milk crate is wedged under a wardrobe mounted on bricks. Inside the crate, wrapped from head to foot in a towel, is Hlamalani, a three-year-old victim of

Second World War veteran George Resenga with five of the fifteen relatives he supports on his meagre pension.
Photograph: Louise Gubb

cerebral palsy. She has begun to whimper at the sound of voices but cannot move because of her paralysing affliction. Linda pulls the crate out from under the cupboard and lifts Hlamalani out.

The disturbance wakes another huddled body lying alone in a corner alongside the wardrobe. Her face is covered in mucus, her eyes wide with fright. She is nine-year-old Tsakani, a retarded child. Linda says she was an entirely normal little girl, laughing and chattering, until the age of four, when she was raped by the 18-year-old son of a neighbour. Since then she has not spoken a word. Tsakani sleeps alone because she bites the other children, even while sleeping. 'She is like an animal,' says Linda.

Tsakani and Hlamalani are sisters. Soon after Hlamalani's birth their mother left home, unable to face life with two disabled children. Nobody knows where she went.

George, a chronic asthmatic, has a room to himself because he is frequently awakened in the night, especially in winter, by blocked bronchial tubes that leave him heaving and gasping for breath.

The whole household is rising now, except George who has had a bad night. Linda heard him coughing and retching for an hour or more. 'He's very sick,' she says as she washes steel plates from the previous night's meal. George's other daughter, Grace, is reheating maize porridge left over from supper. Cockroaches and other insects scurry up the discoloured, peeling wall beside the stove. The children will scoop up a handful of the clogged porridge and eat it on the way to school; it is the only food they will have until supper time. Known as pap or phuthu, it is black South Africa's staple diet. The Resenga family eats it at every meal, with the occasional addition of a relish, and meat once in a while.

A cock crows inside the house. Linda, standing in front of the bathroom door, pushes it open with her foot, revealing thirteen white hens and a shrieking orange rooster. A bad smell escapes from within: the place is a mess of excrement. The chickens perch on the bath and stare from the dark room. 'It is not safe to leave them outside at night,' explains Linda. 'They will be stolen.' She and her sister sell the eggs to raise a little more income for the family; they cannot afford to eat the protein themselves.

When the children are dressed, they file outside to wash in large basins of water that Linda has warmed in a bucket on the coal stove. A small hut in the backyard houses a lavatory made from an upturned wooden crate with a hole at the top.

Inside the house, the furniture has been returned to its daytime positions in the living room. 'Jesus is Lord' says a placard on the wall. A faded print of a dusky woman, peering seductively from under the brim of a black hat, is hanging beside it. The head of the household enters, looking dishevelled, but he is willing to talk about his life.

* * *

George Resenga is a man of humble means and towering dignity. Born in 1915 in a village called Sibasa in the Northern Transvaal, he absorbed his values in the years before the white people of South Africa viewed blacks as a dangerous threat to be controlled and harassed at all costs. Educated to a level of basic literacy in a mission school established at the turn of the century, he learnt at the feet of Catholic priests to be tolerant, well mannered and obedient to God's laws.

George is the only one of his household who can read and write. He is also the only one to have held a steady job, as a cashier in a beer-hall in Soweto from 1946 to 1979. Before that he served in South Africa's defence force for five years, as a medical orderly with the Native Military Corps in Egypt during World War Two.

'Some of us joined the army to get jobs but I joined for happiness, because I wanted to be a soldier and help people all over the world to get rid of this bad thing, the Nazis. I was taking temperatures, washing patients, feeding them, digging graves. Sometimes when I was on ambulance duty we collected wounded and dead soldiers from the battlefield, many of them, crying and screaming. It makes your heart sick for a few days but then you must forget it.

'It was hard, very hard in the army, working like a machine all day and into the night. And hot, very hot in the desert near Cairo. But I was happy: I just liked to help the soldiers. It's where I learnt to be kind to a sick person. When my wife passed away in 1987, I helped her. I knew she was dying from cancer but I was not afraid. She told me I was the angel of mercy; that is the last thing she said before she passed away.

'I am glad I learnt to help people in my life. At the time when I came to Johannesburg in 1935, when it was very hard to live in the location — dirty water running everywhere, children sick and dying, twenty families in one yard, no jobs — every African helped the other, even strangers. Now some still help, there and there, but most can help only themselves.

'Before the war, the trouble in the location was drinking. The people were brewing their own beer behind the houses and drinking, all the time drinking and quarrelling with each other. Then the police would come and take them away. It was OK; only family quarrels there and there but no guns, no black politicians, no army tanks shooting into houses. That started later.

'In 1948, when the Nationalists took over from General Smuts, the laws changed. When the pass laws came, the police were very strict. They made the trouble, not the people. That is why the Africans started to get angry: more and more angry every year.

'Today, family life in Soweto is much different. There are too many women who are not married; too many men who are not married. Too many children have got no mothers and fathers. They all care about themselves, not others. Too many steal because they can't find jobs.

'When it is hot inside the house, you can't sleep in the yard under the sky in Soweto any more because the tsotsis are running all over at night. They look for money, jackets, anything they come across, to sell. Or they kill you for nothing, maybe just for fun, because they are drinking and smoking dagga (marijuana). The dagga is the real leader of the young people of Soweto, not the politicians. If they are smoking dagga, they are not afraid of anything. They will come to you with a knife or a gun or a panga. They do not respect anybody, not the old people, the police or the politicians.

'I remember when it started to get bad in 1976. I went to work at the beer-hall in Pimville on 17 June and the sky was black with smoke. All night, the schoolchildren had been running around, burning and looting. The beer-hall was OK but I didn't know if I should open the door or keep it locked. I waited and saw a crowd coming. I just stood outside and watched them. I couldn't run away because I was the one in charge of the beer-hall. Then they started to throw stones and bottles. One rock hit me. I saw a police van on the other road but the children ran at it, throwing stones, and it turned around and drove off. I thought if the police have run away it is time for me to run also. I took off my dustcoat and locked the door. But I didn't run; I walked away slowly. I was thinking that these young ones must not believe the old ones are afraid of them. But I was afraid.'

George's 19-year-old grandson, also named George, has just left the house. As the front door closes behind him, the old man says: 'I am afraid of him, my own grandson. He takes dagga. He is going now to meet his friends and smoke. He gives a lot of trouble, stealing things to get money. The police have arrested him twice. They keep him in the cell for a few days and let him go. He is a tsotsi. I know because I see the things he steals — radios, watches. He is a tsotsi but I cannot say he is no good because he is still my grandson. When your finger is sore, you can't say it's not my finger any more and cut it off; it is still your finger.

'Every house in Soweto has the same problems. Next door, the teenagers went for armed robbery. One of them killed a white man. The police arrested him. They sentenced him to death. It was the father who called the police, when he heard that his son had killed somebody. He said, no, I will not hide my son who has committed murder. The father talked to me before he went to the police and I advised him the same as he advised himself; go to the police. When they called the parents to Pretoria to see the son before they hanged him, the father went but the mother couldn't go. Both of them loved the son, a murderer; they couldn't help it. The father cried so much in Pretoria and after he returned. The mother got sick. She stayed in her bed, turned to the wall. She died just after the day her son was hanged.

'The trouble in Soweto is education: we have not enough education. The young ones cannot get jobs because there is nothing they can do without education. They can only fight over the bones of what other people have caught in their lives. All my children and grandchildren are sick in their hearts because they want what other people, white people, have got.

I wish I had died before my wife because I think she was better than me at telling these children not to be so angry. I cannot tell them; I don't know what to say.

'I just tell them that everyone must believe in God, whether they go to church or not. The young people of Soweto never go to church. They say God helps only the people with money, the white people. I say, no, it's the money that helps the whites, not God. God never created money. Some blacks get rich, there and there, and some stay poor.

'The animals are waiting for rain so that they can eat grass. When the rain comes, they're living OK. They don't need money to buy grass. My children have food. They are hungry sometimes but they are not starving so they should not have so much hate in their hearts. God put us on earth to see what we can do. If we make mistakes it is our fault, not God's. My daughters tell me they pray to God for money but they don't get it. I never pray for money. I pray to live until the day it was marked in heaven that I should die, and then I will die. I must try to be happy, every day, and not worry too much. If you worry and feel angry, you will steal or drink or smoke dagga. And then your life is over.

'But my children and their children do not think the same way. I am wondering what will happen to them all when I die and there is no money in this house. The older ones will have to work or go to jail. But the younger ones, those that are not even ready for school yet; what will happen to them? What about Hlamalani; who has money and time for a person that cannot walk and talk? I can't help them when I am dead but all the time I'm asking myself what will happen. There is no answer.'

2

Getting Even

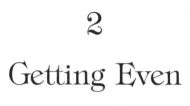

It is 5.30 on a Wednesday evening. The heat of the day hangs oppressively in a small room tightly packed with young men and a few boys, fourteen of them, talking and yelling at each other and jostling as if in a shower room after a football match. A television set blares on a footstool wedged in a corner; it is swaying a bit from the vibrations of kicking legs.

The youths sprawl on to the floor. Some lounge on tatty chairs, sitting on one another's laps and on the arm rests. Two engage in a wrestling contest, their bodies lurching against others who protest irritably. A middle-aged woman, the tenant of the house, appears in the doorway, looking pained and making calming gestures with her hands, but they take no notice. As she retreats, the youths hiss for silence. Every eye is now trained on the television.

It is time for *The Bold and the Beautiful*, a Hollywood soap opera screened daily in South Africa. Typical of its genre, the show features immaculately groomed men and women engaged in various modes of hedonism and revenge in exotic locations. The black youths of Soweto are transfixed. On the screen is a blonde beauty lying in a cool white hospital bed, her eyes brimful with tears as she utters declarations of love to her suave husband. The scene cuts to another bed, this time containing the naked body of the same man romping with a different, equally lovely woman. The camera pans briefly around their stylish celluloid love nest, picking up symbols of wealth and luxury — a magnum of champagne in a giant silver ice bucket, an art treasure displayed on a marble plinth, jewels casually strewn over the dressing table. Then the action moves to a polished mahogany boardroom, where a silver-haired tycoon is plotting the demise of his business partner.

It is a half-hour programme which seems to end all too soon for the mesmerised youths. The room reeks with the smell of atshitshi (marijuana). As the credits roll on to the screen and the familiar signature tune plays out, they sit in silence for a while. A leg stretches out to punch the television's transmission switch. Though the screen is blank, still they stare at it, reluctant to stir from the spell. Slowly, stretching cramped limbs, they begin to rise and the din of talk and shouting envelops the room once more.

But the mood has changed. Sullen and suspicious, most of the youths file out into the street, gathering in the fading light to plan the night's activities. Some — including an aggressive 16-year-old who is repeating phata-phata, meaning sex, in a monotonous, drugged tone — walk off to visit girlfriends. Some go home in hope of a meal. Others stroll to a nearby shebeen to drink beer. Three are left in the street, standing together, speaking in quiet voices for a long time. A few linger in the room, still willing to talk as arranged.

It is dark now and the figures of the youths outside are shadowy in the dim light cast by a lone street lamp. They are planning ukuspina, meaning 'to spin'. 'It is when you go to steal,' explains a youth in the house, who knows of their plans. 'All of us do this when we need money. We can steal cars, or from shops. Anywhere there is dulas (loot) we can take it. They will go to a white part of Johannesburg when it is late. They can hire a car and also guns if they do not have them. These magitas (guys) have guns. I myself have a gun. It is my helping hand.

'They will drive in the white man's streets, looking for a house or a car. They are thinking about *The Bold and the Beautiful*; all that is going on in the beautiful houses where the whites have too much money, everything, and we black dogs have nothing. That is why we watch *The Bold and the Beautiful*. It reminds us how much the whites have got. It gives us strength and courage to spin and maybe rape, ya man. Ek wil eet (I want to eat). I must steal to get money. I don't want to die from malnutrition. I'd rather die a hero, stealing a car, supporting my family. Hey, man, it's OK. If we have to start (shoot) them, we will do it. We are not scared.'

Another youth offers an explanation for his friend's casual threat of murder and rape. 'We do not go looking for to hurt somebody. But we must be prepared. If it comes to the push, I shoot. It's survival of the fittest. If you don't shoot, you end up in jail — or dead. I never had a white woman. It is something I am thinking about. If a white woman looks at you as a dog, shakes her king-size ezzies (buttocks) and walks away, that is when you say I am not just a galpil darkie (useless black). I can have power over you and nothing can stop me, even your money, even your white skin. That is why you rape them; when they snob you.'

A third youth, aged 22, is rolling a marijuana cigarette, known as a zoll or a fuse. His eyes are red and glazed. He explains that he has served two terms of imprisonment for hausa (house-breaking and theft). 'Tonight I can take a car, go to Diepkloof, fight with a gang — knives, not guns — because I don't need to spin now. Not tonight. I got a Toyota in Pretoria on Monday. I sold it to a clever (a hardened, admired criminal).

A youth smokes a 'white pipe', a blend of marijuana and mandrax inhaled through the top of a broken beer bottle.
Photograph: Victor Matom

We arranged it the same day because iya shisa (it was hot). He paid me and my friend R3 000.

'I know this is dirty money but I need it. I am trying to save myself and my children. If you haven't got education, what must you do? You must use your brains to steal. Yeh, man. Hai! The most important thing in life is money. Money makes the world go round. I know a girl in Soweto who went to university but she can't get a job because she is black. Instead of sitting under a tree smoking dagga we'd rather be doing something else but what can we do? I can't go back to school to learn with my younger sister. It is making me ashamed to sit in school like a big sissy boy with the younger children. So I must steal. It is not good. It is a shit life and I am a coward. But we always smoke dagga first, before we spin. It relaxes you, especially with mandrax, and makes you powerful from the anger. We have that anger, all of us here in Soweto. It is only the rich black people, the amahaiza (snobs), who do not have that anger. They have forgotten where they came from and we will steal from them also, the same as the whites. Yeh, man. Hai!'

A 19-year-old with a prison record walks into the room. He is peeling an orange with a long knife. Its sharpened blade gleams menacingly as he halts, much too close for normal discourse. 'Are you scared?' he asks. The others in the room howl with laughter. A fresh zoll is doing the rounds. The youths draw deeply on it with their eyes closed, dreamy expressions accompanying their hard words.

'When we go to a house to steal in the night and somebody catches us, we must shoot. They say they will not call the police but they will, we know that, as soon as we run away they call the police. One says he has no gun but he shoots when you are running away. All whites have guns, like us. We are even. We take their things. The insurance will pay them for what we take.

'If there is a burglar alarm in the house, we can switch it off. We know how to do these things. The very ones who are installing them are teaching us how to dismantle them. If there is a dog at the house, it's OK. You look into the eyes of the dog and it will go away. Or if it attacks, you knife it. Sometimes we can put a small, dead dog in the fridge — or in the oven, and then turn it on. When that woman comes home, she smells her dog in the oven. Man, she cries! It's revenge because she likes her dog more than us. You can see when she buys food for her dog from Woolworths; compare the price with the food she buys for her maid. Hai!'

One of the youths jumps to his feet and motions to the others. 'The tsotsis are going,' he says and they all depart abruptly. Outside in the night, they laugh and shout, pushing each other playfully as teenagers do when there is no better way to expend energy. Their twisted, antisocial attitudes seem all the more grotesque when viewed against the youthful exuberance which shines momentarily in the moonlight as they saunter away, laughing lustily, with their arms affectionately intertwined.

*   *   *

The lifestyles adopted during the 1980s by the youth of Soweto and most other South African townships are frightening by any standards. Brutalised thugs range in age from ten to twenty-four years, a group which is collectively termed 'youth' in South Africa and constitutes one-third of the country's population.

Deep lines of alienation have been carved in the minds and hearts of many, probably most, of the nation's seven million youths by discriminatory social policies enshrined in laws that actively undermined black family life; by the resentment of those who could not be educated; by the despair of parents who moved daily between squalor at home and a menial job;

by the mounting conviction that apartheid could be resolved only through violence.

The two major factors in the socialisation of a healthy adult — the family and the educational system — have both suffered severe upheaval for decades and have failed lamentably in the crucial process of nurturing constructive values in the young. 'My father left home when I was six. He went to the mines to work,' says a 19-year-old. 'In the beginning he sent us money for food and clothing; then after a year or so the money stopped coming. We did not know what happened. Then some people came back and told me that he spent all his money on women and in the shebeens (night clubs) with his friends. Then my brother and my mother went (to the city) to work. I was alone with my brothers and sisters at home. There was no mother, no father; what could I do? I went to school for two years, then I dropped out and now I do nothing. No one was around when I needed them.'

Many youths like this one have opted for life in political or criminal street gangs, not only to escape from unsupportive families in overcrowded homes, but to find status and security.

In seeking alternatives to the school and the family, Soweto's youths first explored the political culture of the late 1970s and 1980s, involving demonstrations, school boycotts, burning, stoning and other forms of politically legitimate violence. Known as comrades and directed by well-trained leaders, the politically motivated youth were in the vanguard of the liberation struggle. It was they who struck the first persuasive blow to apartheid in the student uprisings that began in 1976, leading to the empowerment of the ANC's military wing, and it was they who waged the popular uprisings known as 'people's war' that erupted throughout South Africa's townships between 1984 and 1986. Many were forced into hiding and exile; others were maimed or killed.

'From the perspective of the youth, this was a time of euphoria as well as terror,' says Professor Gill Straker, a psychologist and author of *Faces in the Revolution*. 'They had a newfound sense of power and a vision for the future. They saw themselves as leading the older generation to freedom. Liberation was believed to be in sight and they were to be the authors of it.'

In the heady process of consolidating the power they had first experienced in the students' revolt of 1976, black youths learnt to commit and live with violence on a daily basis. Many developed a frightening belief upon which they acted: that they were going to die and did not care. War and insurrection were the slogans of the day; courage and recklessness characterised their actions.

But when the country's political direction changed from confrontation to negotiation following the unbanning of the ANC in 1990, many comrades had difficulty adapting to the new environment. Their lives in the townships did not improve, yet their leaders no longer advocated insurrection. The youths became bored with having nothing to do but smoke marijuana, drink beer and dream of better days that might never come. Discipline within the organised youth movements began to deteriorate as a result of inactivity and demotivated leadership. Some simply lost interest in politics; others became more militant. A typically hostile reaction is that of a comrade who pays lip service to the idea of negotiations but has little faith in the process because he feels that his 'forefathers tried talking for decades, but achieved nothing . . . I believe in fighting and fighting until we are free. Even if I die I feel it will be worth while if I have achieved something before then that will benefit those who remain behind.'

A number of former comrades express outright bitterness towards the political leaders they once admired. 'In 1986 they told us not to write exams and we obeyed. We were throwing stones for the struggle, risking our lives, running from the police, not living at home. Then we realised that the leaders' children were safely at school across the border in Swaziland, passing their exams when we were dying in the streets of Soweto. Before, we thought liberation was around the corner and we would have jobs, somewhere to live. But we were wrong. Now we struggle only for ourselves. We steal to have smart clothes and something to eat and to help our own families, not the families of the struggle.'

Establishing a career on the wrong side of the law is not a new notion in Soweto. Many local heroes since the 1950s have been gangsters with long criminal records. Some of Soweto's richest black businessmen − role models for the youth − proudly admit to earlier lives of crime, forgiving themselves all sins on the grounds that oppression precluded legitimate options. But the belief that it is possible to become rich without ever finding conventional employment is now so widespread that the job market is openly scorned by thousands of youths. 'Who needs to work when you can steal a BMW and live from that every month?' asks an expensively dressed 21-year-old.

Where the tsotsis acknowledge their immorality is in their concept of umlalaphantsi, meaning 'a big break', through which they hope to be rescued from crime. It symbolises the naive belief that they will eventually accumulate a large amount of money with which to set up lucrative businesses and thus be rich and respectable. A 20-year-old, asked if he went to church, replied: 'Not these days. I cannot go to church because I am a thief. But I can't always be a thief because the younger ones must take over. They can run faster. I can go to church when I get umlalaphantsi.'

Soweto's political and criminal youth cultures merge uncomfortably in the subculture of the comtsotsis (comrade/ tsotsi) — youths who are often barely politically literate but who attempt to justify their antisocial behaviour as legitimate political activity. The cynical comtsotsis use political overtures to limit risk, not to make their criminal activities more morally acceptable to themselves or others. 'If you are a comtsotsi, you can take from the community and pretend you want it for the struggle,' explains a youth of this persuasion. 'You can run into a house in Soweto where there is a car and say, "Come comrades, lend me your car. I have to go to a funeral with Comrade Mandela." They give you the keys because they must help the struggle. But you don't bring it back. You take that car and spin and spin and spin.

'You can also sometimes hijack an ambulance: tell the driver to get out because you need it for the struggle, to rescue somebody. Then you use the ambulance to rob, even a bank, because it is a safe getaway vehicle.

'The real comrades are very much angry with the comtsotsis because they give the struggle a bad name. There is very much fighting between comrades and comtsotsis, big battles in the streets, here in Soweto, where people die from knives and guns. Hai! Sometimes the tsotsis want to teach the comrades a lesson. Sometimes it is the comrades who come to kill the tsotsis. Fighting, all the time fighting. Man, it is a dangerous life.'

Not all the young people who join gangs in Soweto do so for political or criminal ends. There are a number of other social groups, such as the Mapantsulas, whose members base their identity on fashion, music and a unique style of dance. In some cases, members of the Mapantsula, Rastafarian or Jazz sub-cultures are also linked to criminal gangs that are, like Soweto's Zebra Force or the Godfathers, modelled on American gangster movies in which 'the bad guys win, get rich, smash the cops, and live happily ever after', as one youth expressed his cult ideal.

* * *

Reggie Nthoba used to be one of Soweto's most infamous gang leaders. For six years he and three other tsotsis, calling themselves the Amajapan, stole vehicles in Johannesburg and Pretoria, sometimes at the rate of three a night. They specialised in late model Japanese cars and trucks.

So slick were the Amajapan that criminals operating 'body shops', in which stolen vehicles are stripped of identification, used to order specific models for waiting clients and pay Reggie upfront for them. He received around R5 000 for each vehicle, a fraction of their true value because the cars were in the Amajapan's possession for only a few hours before passing further into the underworld.

In March 1989, Reggie recruited a new gang member who turned out to be a police informer. The Amajapan were arrested and sent to prison.

While in jail, Reggie became sick. His strength ebbed slowly away until the prison doctors realised he was seriously ill and sent him for specialist diagnosis.

The verdict was a massive tumour on the spine. 'They told me it was inoperable,' said Reggie matter-of-factly during an interview. 'They said I did not have long to live. But that was a year ago and I'm living better now, even though I'm quadriplegic and I can only move my head, than in my whole life before. This illness took something away — my body — but it has given me the boldness to survive through my spirit, by helping others instead of cheating and robbing.'

A brief, heroic chapter in Reggie's life story began several months after his illness was diagnosed, when he was released from prison. 'I sat in the wheelchair for many days and thought about my sad state. Then one morning I saw a crippled man dragging himself along the street outside my father's house, where I stay. I thought to myself, "There must be many, many people like that in these houses, with no one to help them." That idea was in my mind, day after day, while I sat with nothing to do.

'Then I had a good thought. I decided to put an advertisement in the *Sowetan*, asking volunteers to come forward and help me do research among the disabled. I waited for the day when it was in the newspaper, and waited for the telephone to ring. It began ringing late in the morning, and then it never stopped. I recruited twenty-eight volunteers, most of them girls. They also shared my thought: to help disabled people who cannot help themselves and do not have families with people working, like I have a father with a job, lucky for me.'

One of the volunteers, a quiet 20-year-old named Salome, became Reggie's devoted minder. She fed him small meals every four hours as the doctors advised; she was usually on hand to thump his chest when he needed to clear his lungs but had no strength to cough; she brought a jam jar to his aid when he needed to relieve his bladder, discreetly shielding his body from view with her wide skirt because she was not strong enough to lift him on to the lavatory. 'Reggie's friends don't mind if we do this without leaving the room,' she explained. 'And it's difficult to get the wheelchair into the bathroom.'

'I had many meetings with the volunteers and we made a plan,' Reggie's voice continued from behind Salome's skirt. 'We went from house to house, knocking on four hundred doors in the first plan, and asking if there were disabled people inside. It took a long time because the girls had to push my wheelchair and also make notes because I cannot write. We tried to help some of the disabled on the spot. Hai! There is too much suffering in those houses. People dirty, smelling, with septic wounds from lying too long in bed, and no food, sometimes locked up in the house alone all day; very, very sad people. I told my volunteers what to do: bath this one, clean that wound, feed this one. We didn't have money to buy many things but we had Dettol and some bandages and some things to eat. Then we left some of the volunteers at that house and went on to the next one.

'At the end, we had notes on two hundred and seventy-three disabled people. I phoned Baragwanath Hospital but they told me they cannot come to the houses. The people must come to the hospital or to a clinic. But most of these people have no money for a taxi and they cannot walk. How can they get there?

'Some of the volunteers began to lose hope and a few of them left. But I kept on phoning, talking to this one and that one. Then I talked to the head of the social work department at Baragwanath and she said, "OK: what we can do is give your volunteers some training so they can help the disabled better."

'So then we became more effective as care-givers. We are also raising some funds from overseas to buy equipment and provide care for the handicapped. Our programme is going very well.

'My friends are still the tsotsis I used to steal cars with, and the ones I met in prison. They all know me. My younger brother is a gang leader, and all the ones he spins with respect me, even though I am a sissy boy now. I was a big man in the world of crime before my sickness. Amajapan was famous in Soweto, hai! They (the tsotsis) accept what I do now and I accept what they do. A hungry man will do anything; he has no choice. There is a better way to live and I have found it. But these others are not so lucky.'

Reggie's 'luck' ran out at midnight on 27 December 1992, when the random violence which is so rife in Soweto struck within his own family. Salome, who often slept at the Nthoba home and had become a member of the household, was searching for her deodorant prior to taking a bath. Reggie told her he had seen his younger brother, Thamodi, using it. Salome called out the brother's name, thinking he was outside the house smoking 'white pipes' (dagga and mandrax) with his friends in the moonlight.

When he failed to respond, Reggie suggested she look in the bedroom Thamodi shared with other members of the family. She was shuffling through his belongings when the drugged 21-year-old youth rushed in behind her, demanding to know what she was doing. When Salome replied that Reggie had told her to look among his things for the missing deodorant, Thamodi charged from the room and attacked his crippled brother.

Salome heard Reggie's cries in the sitting-room and ran to help him. The crazed youth, having flung Reggie out of his wheelchair, was kicking his brother's wasted body around the floor. Salome tried to intervene. Thamodi drew a knife from his pocket and stabbed her through the heart. She died instantly.

Reggie was taken to hospital. Internal injuries from the assault had devastated his already frail body. His life was still hanging in the balance at the time of writing.

* * *

Among the ugliest developments in Soweto's growing gangsterism is the emergence of the youth subculture of violence known as 'jackrolling'. The word was coined in reference to the forceful abduction of women in Soweto by a gang called Jackrollers, which began with ten members led by a youth named Jeff Brown. He revelled in his reputation as the most feared man in the township. Rape, car theft and bank robbery

Sowetan youths pose for the camera after an interview with the author. In the centre is Reggie Nthoba.
Photograph: Louise Gubb

were the Jackrollers' objectives, and they terrorised Soweto for several years before being killed, probably by comrades. Though utterly feared by women in Soweto, the Jackrollers were admired by some male youths to the extent that the abduction of women became fashionable during their violent reign. Long after the demise of the original gang, those who abduct and rape are proud to call themselves jackrollers.

The few studies that have been undertaken in Soweto on marginalised youth have tended to focus on crimes like robbing, stealing and the violence that often attends such activities. But the experience of social alienation encompasses the whole person, not only his/her material aspirations. The acute sense of powerlessness that prevails among South Africa's black youths encroaches on other spheres of life, such as sexual attitudes. Rape is common in Soweto. A symbolic reassertion of power, it yields psychological rewards in a culture steeped in beliefs of aggressive male supremacy.

Men, including whites in the dominant South African machismo culture, have learnt to define their power in terms of their ability to effect their will, without the consent of others. This is often displayed in the attitudes of young black males towards sex.

Asked to describe his reaction when a girl refused to have sex, one youth replied: 'You see, I have told myself that "cherries" can't tell me anything. When I want it, she must give. You see, girls think they are clever sometimes. She will make excuses, claiming she is sick, and all that. I make it clear that when I want it, I want it now. If you are soft and you let her get away with it, you will not get her.' Another youth said: 'Hai! No ways she likes it or not. She has to give it.'

The vocabulary used by many Sowetan youths to describe sex is in itself revealing of the link between sexuality and violence:

ukuhlaba (to stab), uku peita (to spray), ugushaya nge kauza (to hit her with the pipe). Describing the typical sexual attitude of township magitas, one youth said: 'You can see from the way he carries himself when he walks out of the house. He will be smiling and walking proudly. The girl will be looking on the ground. He will have humbled her. She will come back walking with her thighs apart because the "thing" is sore.'

A characteristic of jackrolling is the rapists' failure to conceal their criminal deeds: part of the exercise is to be seen jackrolling, so as to earn respect among peers. Most of these rapes are committed in daylight and in public places like shebeens and schools, or in the streets. Jackrolling is widely viewed by the youths of Soweto as the sport of tough and respected gangsters. 'It is not a crime,' said one teenager. 'It is just a game.'

Just as the jackrollers' vile deeds are deliberately committed in full view of the community, so was the death in 1990 of one of the most feared rapists in Soweto, a brutal young man known as Tebogo. He added a cruel dimension to jackrolling by publicly humiliating his victims before raping them. Terrified, weeping young women would be forced to dance on table tops or crawl around in circles for hours while Tebogo taunted them with a knife or a gun, and urinated on them.

As the community grew more and more incensed by Tebogo's crimes, Soweto's comrades decided to hunt for the hated villain and kill him. It took many months to trap Tebogo but when they finally stabbed him to death, the comrades were determined to publicise their revenge. They hacked off the head of the corpse and impaled it on a pole for all to see. A crowd of children sang and danced around Tebogo's severed head. Adults threw stones at the grisly trophy until the police arrived to remove it.

3

Crisis in the Classroom

▼▼▼

M urphy Morobe is standing on a concrete foundation slab, all that remains of his first classroom at Morris Isaacson High School in Central Western Jabavu. The walls were smashed over the years by successive brigades of angry students. The bricks, window frames, doors, roofing, ceiling, blackboard, desks and chairs have been carried away by squatters gathering building materials for their shacks.

'There are conflicting demands and interests in this community,' says Morobe, a leader in Morris Isaacson's 'Class of '76', which led the historic Soweto students' uprising of 16 June that year. 'The people outside these school gates are looking for homes: they don't have anywhere to live. Schools stand empty for long periods during boycotts. There's no education but people see corrugated iron for roofs and chairs to sit on. So there's this natural phenomenon in Soweto: if something is standing there not being used, it will be put to a better — or worse — use. Whether that's right or wrong is another matter, but it's a fact which requires some understanding.'

We stroll around the derelict buildings of South Africa's most famous black school. Some classrooms without roofs are still in use. Others have gaping holes in the walls. The science laboratory is an empty shell, with two walls and the roof missing. 'In our day the building was intact but there was never any equipment; it was always due but never came,' says Morobe, a prominent United Democratic Front (alias ANC) politician during the 1980s and today a respected corporate businessman. 'That didn't stop a number of guys from the "Class of '76" becoming doctors and dentists. We learnt physics by rote, memorising book descriptions of experiments we'd never seen. Dr Gordon Sibiya, South Africa's only black nuclear physicist, was educated at Morris Isaacson.'

The dilapidated buildings are daubed with graffiti: 'The people shall govern', 'Away with school inspectors'. Children wander in and out of the school grounds at a time of day when they should be attending lessons. Morobe greets a group of students, walking in single file along a well-worn path. One of them raises his fist in the black power salute.

'That's the path we used when we wanted to bunk classes in order to attend a Black Consciousness meeting or go to a movie with a girlfriend — or run away from the cops. It used to lead to a hole in the fence but the entire fence has now disappeared.

'This is where the school hall used to be. It was wrecked long ago. It's where we said the Lord's Prayer every morning of our lives — until 16 June 1976. That morning we sang "Nkosi Sikelel' iAfrika" for the first time. It was the first inkling our teachers had that something was about to happen. It took them completely by surprise because we'd managed to keep our plans secret. We then marched out of the school's entrance over there and down the road, where we collected another procession from a neighbouring school, then another secondary school joined us, and so on, towards Dube, past Crossroads, right through Soweto. It was a great experience for all of us.

'The most formative steps in my political development were taken within these school walls, beginning around 1974, when we organised pro-Frelimo rallies, celebrated the demise of the Portuguese in Mozambique and the coup in Portugal. Those events made a big impression on us because we realised the white man in Africa could be defeated.

'I came to Isaacson every morning at 7 from my home in Orlando East, which is quite far away. I had the option of going to a closer school but Isaacson in those days had a good reputation as a learning institution, in spite of the difficulties of Bantu Education. Many of us aspired to finding places at this school. With only about ten secondary schools in Soweto at that time, they screened applicants because there was such a demand for places. The staff were strict in terms of discipline and very clearly focused in terms of academic achievement. When I was accepted, due to the good marks I'd achieved the previous year, I was very happy.

'My parents were ordinary workers, who were very concerned about education. Most black parents were in those days. We had a reasonable family life, nothing special, no money, but we got the things we needed most. We were only allowed to leave school at 5 o'clock and then we had to rush home to do our chores. I had to clean the kitchen and light the fire: it was my responsibility. At 7.00 p.m., having done the household chores and my homework and eaten supper, I'd walk all the way back to school from Orlando power station, where I lived. There, until about 10 o'clock, we'd work in a study group organised by ourselves. Nobody told us to do it: we wanted to learn.

'It was tough getting a good education in those days, but some of us managed it. I look at the "Class of '76" to see where they are today. Many have made a significant impact on the wider community outside Soweto; people like educationalists

Fanyana Mazibuko and Lucas Ngakane, and doctors like Cecil Manitshane, who is the chairperson of the National Medical and Dental Association. A number of us ended up as political prisoners on Robben Island. Many went into exile and studied abroad.'

Several pupils who led the 1976 schools revolt, including Murphy Morobe, recently formed the Morris Isaacson High School Alumni Association, a support group which hopes to reconstruct the school's buildings and inspire students to 'realise that they have been in a war, but now they have to be debriefed,' according to Fanyana Mazibuko, head of the Alumni Association's ten-man committee.

'What is true for Morris Isaacson is true for every black school in Soweto,' says Morobe. 'But obviously, for us, the place to begin is where we suckled as youngsters. I come here and reflect on the tradition of Morris Isaacson, which was well known for its academic prowess long before '76. If the parents of today's pupils looked back at what Isaacson used to be, all would agree it's what they'd like the school to rise up and become again.'

He greets several students and a teacher as they pass. 'A lot of them know me through my political career. Or, in the case of teachers, because they were here at school with me seventeen years ago. A spirit survives, in spite of the battered buildings and the very low academic standards; a sense of spiritual continuity, which we would like to enhance.

'The possibility exists to create a bond between those of us who were here before and those who are suffering through the dereliction which has since taken place. For me, that is an important challenge. If we could make this school pulsate again and achieve the academic excellence of 1976... It's useful to entertain ideas about how we'll reconstruct the school, and hopefully we'll find a receptive group of alumni to translate those ideas into action. I suppose we're all waiting for champions to rise up among us and lead such reconstruction projects. Or perhaps it's more a challenge for political organisations than local communities.

'I would never suggest coming to the school and simply putting in equipment. It would all be vandalised, as has happened in the past. What has to happen here concerns the community. Reconstruction can't be done by outsiders. You need not only to reconstruct the buildings but also the concept of the school. I wouldn't pull in an outside contractor. I'd go around each of these houses, all of them containing more than one person who's unemployed. Some will have building experience. Mobilise them, and the parents whose children could some day excel at the school, and let them be part of raising the phoenix from the ashes.

'For me, the challenge of Morris Isaacson is finding a way to rekindle the learning culture that once thrived here. You can see by the way the students are strolling about aimlessly, a month from exams, that they're not going to pass. You're looking at a generation, generations, that will never hold together socially because they have no stability, no discipline, no employment prospects at all, which is tragic.

'I don't know each one of these students we see passing by but, in the Soweto context, it's not difficult to imagine where they will be in five years' time. Crime is the obvious call for a lot of them, alcoholism, drug abuse, teenage pregnancies: all the last resorts of hopelessness. And this scene is duplicated all over the country; students not learning, teachers not teaching.'

We pass three teachers gossiping in the sun. One of them tells us she is resting because only five students turned up for her lesson. Why didn't she teach the five? She shrugs off the

A new Soweto generation hopes for better educational opportunities than were available to black children in the past.

Photograph: Victor Matom

question, a coy smile illuminating her pretty face as she continues to file her fingernails.

'Every time I come here I leave with a heavy heart, seeing what's happened, or rather what's not happening. My dream is for Morris Isaacson — where the revolution began in 1976 (that's how we saw it at the time, as the big moment, the start of the revolution) — to be the place, the centre where reconstruction of education begins in 1994. It's an important symbolism. If reconstruction can happen here, it can happen anywhere and everywhere. It's got to start somewhere. Individuals can do it to some extent, in individual schools. If you take one school, the project is achievable, whereas if you're looking at reconstructing education in the whole of Soweto, or the whole of South Africa, it's a daunting prospect.'

* * *

A formidable task lies ahead if the gap between black and white primary and secondary schooling is to be bridged in South Africa. An estimated 45 000 extra classrooms will have to be built nationwide. An even greater number of properly qualified teachers will have to be provided because virtually all existing schools in black townships are chronically under-staffed. Since the state already allocates over 20 per cent of its total budget to education — the largest allocation to a single sector — a new logic in distributing existing resources will have to be found if parity in education is to be achieved.

During the 1960s, the black population's annual production of Standard 10s — the last year of secondary schooling — was only 50 per 100 000. This accounts for the fact that, according to an Institute of Race Relations survey conducted in 1979, there were 44 000 black teachers who had not passed Standard 10. Eleven thousand of these had Standard 8 as their highest academic qualification. Such poorly qualified teachers often had to cope with forty-two classes in a week in four different subjects and an average of fifty-five pupils in a class, at a time when the pupil-teacher ratio was 21:1 in white schools.

The situation has barely improved in the years since 1979. About 70 per cent of white pupils today reach matric — the examination required as basic eligibility for most white-collar occupations in South Africa — against 3 per cent of black students. Many matric classes throughout the country are being taught by teachers with scant training: having passed their school examination, they attend a crash course of college lectures and return to township classrooms to teach students writing the same exam. Although the views of the man who created Bantu Education in 1953, Dr Hendrik Verwoerd, have long been an embarrassment to many South African whites, the country's education system still reflects his determination to keep 'the natives as hewers of wood and drawers of water . . . to keep them in their place'.

But there are other reasons for the chaos prevailing in African schools. Black children have been used consistently as cannon fodder and their schools as battlegrounds in the struggle for political power. The revolt against apartheid education, which first erupted in Soweto in 1976, has lost direction to the point where many students can no longer distinguish between the campaign for reform and the call of crime. Teaching has become one of the most dangerous vocations in black townships. Attending classes against the decrees of political activists is sometimes so hazardous for students that they sleep at their desks rather than return home at night.

Dozens of Soweto's schools have hit the headlines in recent years for reasons other than academic or sporting achievement. After six Soweto pupils gang-raped a schoolmate, the principal told the girl's mother there was nothing he could do to punish them. When a local radio station ran a talk show on the black education crisis, a teacher from Fidelitas, a Diepkloof high school, phoned in to share his views and nearly lost his life as a result. He spoke about indiscipline, drugs, alcohol abuse and crime. Some of his pupils were listening and alerted the gangster element in the school. When confronted about the things he had said on radio, the teacher's attempt to explain his right to have and to express his own views proved futile. He was stabbed and beaten up so brutally that he spent weeks recovering in hospital.

A teacher from Phefeni Senior Secondary School in Soweto had a similarly close brush with death, soon after pupils had written end-of-year exams. 'A student, known to be a no-hoper in class, came to me while we were marking papers. He apologised for bothering me, saying he was on his way to town and had just popped in to find out how things were going. As he spoke, he produced a lethal-looking hand gun and fiddled with it casually. I got the message. He was telling me that I either made sure he passed or I would suffer the conse-quences. I told him things were going well for him, although I knew he had performed hopelessly. After he left, I fiddled his papers to make sure he passed. I had very little option.'

Against the backdrop of an escalating national catastrophe in African education, many influential black voices are rising in alarm. 'The ugliest aspect of the deepening crisis in black education is the view held by pupils that they are doing someone a favour by going to school,' wrote Soweto journalist Joe Molefe in *The Star*, a Johannesburg newspaper. A recent biting editorial in the country's biggest selling black daily, the *Sowetan*, said: 'The children, some of them guilty of assaulting teachers and dragging other pupils out of classrooms at the point of knives, are the little heroes standing up to oppression. The black community needs to examine this hypocrisy very closely ... while there is a lot wrong with black education and the Department of Education and Training, our children and organisations have a lot to answer for.'

After fourteen years of intermittent school boycotts, four years of little or no schooling as a result of political slogans like 'liberation now, education later', and the current malaise which the Education Policy Unit of the University of the Witwatersrand calls 'a pervasive decay of authority of any kind', 1993's black matric results were as bleak as the previous year's. The results in 1994 are expected to be worse. Thousands more will be jobless and angry. The country will be poised, yet again, to reap the bitter fruits of unresolved discontent.

* * *

The word most often used to describe the state of black education in South Africa since Soweto's bloody students' uprising eighteen years ago — crisis — appears in most of the newspaper headlines written on the subject since 16 June 1976. It is a word that irritates Sibongile (Bongi) Mkhabela, a bouncy social worker employed by the Development Resource Centre in downtown Johannesburg. 'The teachers talk angrily about crisis but they make matters worse by striking for more pay a few weeks before matric students are due to write their final exams; the politicians talk about it and do nothing except encourage the teachers and students to blame everybody but themselves; and, worst of all, the students talk and cry about it, even though most of them have no initiative to learn.

'Everybody comes in with negatives,' she says. 'I wonder where they get so many negatives? If we talked about challenge rather than crisis we might get somewhere in our schools.'

Bongi Mkhabela was a prominent student activist in 1976 at Soweto's Naledi Secondary School, where much of the planning for the Soweto uprising took place. She has remained loyal to the Black Consciousness movement. 'You ask me how I became successful, how I survived poverty, Bantu education and the political turmoil of the mid-seventies? It's a long story,' she says.

'I'm the fifth-born in a family of six children. My mother was a domestic worker, my father a labourer. Mama died in 1970, when I was fourteen. My father earned R20 a month. What's interesting is, whenever I think of home, I remember a very happy place where the poverty, the R20, didn't really matter. I didn't feel then that we had too little.

'My older brother, who is now a big guy in the corporate world, grew up wearing two pairs of trousers, one with holes at the front, the other with holes at the back. He joked about it all the time. We all laughed about things that were genuinely funny; things that people outside the townships would consider sad or pathetic. He had a tough time because he was older and had to help support us. He'd come home from school, grab his sack of peanuts and sell them on the streets of Soweto to make some money. He learnt very early how to be an entrepreneur. He was strong, not weak, even though he was about as poor as you find anyone in Soweto today. He'd go to Westgate station and do his jive there. We'd shout, "Dance, dance", and he'd do this wild aerobic kind of thing and people gave him money for it. Plus, it was fun.

'We grew up in Zola. When you say Zola, my generation remember it as the Wild West, kwa mshayazale they used to call it, meaning "if you find a person, beat that person dead". Guys used to joke about girls from Zola, saying you never stop one of those chicks. I used to play on it. When a boy stopped me and said where are you from, I'd say Zola in a deep voice and he'd pass on.

'Zola was known as a very, very violent community then, but it was a myth. There was violence, yes, but only in the way that there always is in overcrowded places; fights, too much beer, that sort of thing. Zola is known as a very, very violent community now, but it is not a myth any more.

'I never experienced violence in Zola. I was never raped, never attacked. There was no violence in my home; my brothers were never violent. I felt comfortable and secure in Zola. My parents were not educated but they were strong, decent people with good Christian values. My mother was the really strong one, but kind. When we, even my brothers, thought of Mama, we were terrified. The old man was OK, but that woman! She's the one who put us on the straight line.

'When you grow up and have to struggle for things, and have to be honest and decent, you grow up strong. Many, many things, other than suffering, make Soweto what it is. The people who are suffering don't feel it as much as the ones who are talking about it on the outside. You accept your own destiny, unless someone tells you not to accept it, and then you become weak because you're waiting for someone outside to solve your problems. You're not outside looking in; you're there and you have to survive. People who are looking in say, "How do you cope with six children and R20?" You cope. You know how to do it: you have to.

'It is out of this that you become the adult you are, strong or weak. You look at yourself and, if you're strong, you say, "I'm going to make it from this community into the big world out there." A lot of us made it; a lot didn't. Look at the present political leadership today. Most of them come out of the same environment as I do. Most of them had to struggle for education, for survival.

'I look at Soweto today and it's not the same place as it was, not at all. The contrast for me is almost painful. The young people have been taught by politicians to be indignant about everything, about life itself, to blame others for everything that goes wrong, and to wait for miracles from somewhere.

'Take Naledi, my old school. The kids are not lively and adventurous like we were, dashing away from the cops into the school gates, knowing you're safe when you get inside your community, or safe as you'll be as a political activist. Today, they're dashing away from the cops because they've stolen something, not because of their beliefs, and of course the community does not offer them protection.

'1976 was beautiful rather than sad. You saw the collective consciousness of a community, its togetherness; workers, kids, teachers all going the same way forward, together. They may not have had academic ways of articulating where they were going, but they all knew. They knew what was frustrating them: the Bantu Education system. And also, 1976 was fun, jumping around, challenging that system.

'Sometimes my father would say, "Bongi, please, let some-body else do it. I understand it has to be done but you've played your role. Let somebody else take over." And I'd say, "Who would you suggest? Every student has parents who will be as concerned as you are." So he let me go. He knew I had to do it.

'When the violence began in Soweto and townships all over the country in 1984, terrible violence with necklacing and so on, people talked about the legacy of apartheid. I'm very sceptical about this explanation. It's not the legacy of apartheid alone. If it was, 1976 would have been different. It would have been about people hating themselves, as we are seeing in Soweto now. We were not delinquents. We were students eager to learn, frustrated by a system that forced us to study in Afrikaans, gave us set books a few weeks before our exams, gave us teachers without adequate qualifications, and did very, very many things to slow down our education.

'Between '76 and '84, many, many kids became delinquents. When you are faced with delinquent behaviour, what do you do as a sympathetic parent, journalist or politician? You search for excuses and say it's the legacy of apartheid. We didn't steal and rape for fun. This behaviour is the legacy of something else.

'When we were at school we were there to learn. We had to be there at 8.00 and we came an hour earlier. Now the children come when they feel like it. The parents don't make the children arrive on time, the teachers don't do it. Principals who try to make strict rules are threatened by their own students; some have been necklaced for trying to run their schools efficiently. This is delinquent behaviour. Why?

'You have no authority structures left in Soweto. Children are no longer committed to schooling. Parents and teachers are not committed to it. The kids have no respect for any authority whatsoever. Why?

'It isn't because they feel empowered politically, as some people suggest. I've never seen such political naivety as exists among the youth of Soweto today. They can't express themselves in political terms at all. The youth of 1976 could relate to issues and formulate logical plans of action. They'd identify the problem and say, this is what we should do about it. They'd be able to tell you exactly what was wrong with the system and how it affected them. Today's kids can't even grasp the basic truth that, without education, without struggling, day and night if necessary, to pass matric, they can never expect to move ahead. I passed matric in 1976, even though I was a leader of the uprising that year, even though the schools were closed and many of our teachers had resigned.

'Part of the problem lies with the present teachers. The kids have no insight or vision of their future because their teachers have none. When we were at school our teachers were committed to the black child. It was not just a job for them; it was a calling. The kids and teachers shout now for people's education and they'd rather boycott classes than be pragmatic, knowing that boycotts harm the students more than the system. We had people's education to some extent, not perfect, but it allowed us to pass matric. What would happen is the teacher would say, "OK, this is a history class. According to the Boer's textbook, these are the facts. But I'll tell you the other facts which, remember, you must not write in your examination paper." In this way, our teachers conscientised us and so our politicisation was quite sophisticated. We had the chance to debate issues with our teachers. There was a continuous dialogue between the children and the adults. Even if the teacher had only learnt a little bit more than the student in Standard 10, you respected him or her as an adult with more experience of life.

'Respect is an important word. It is important for parents, teachers and principals. Without it they cannot perform their roles in society. In 1976, we knew how to divorce an issue from an individual. When Nelson Mandela came out of prison, he again taught us this important lesson. He did not hate white people as individuals; he hated the system they had created. Kids in Soweto today don't say, "This is my school principal, he's an elder and I must respect him. Even if I don't agree with everything he's saying, I cannot attack him personally." Today, the person and the problem are indivisible in the eyes of these delinquents.

'I think we must go back to 1976 to find the most important cause of the situation which exists in our schools today. Seventy-six did not have heroes. Some of us were student leaders, yes, but not heroes. It was the politicians and the journalists who promoted a few individuals as heroes. Every anniversary of 16 June you see them, including me, yes, on television and in the newspapers: the heroes of the student uprising that changed the course of South African history. But it wasn't the individuals who did it. Nobody said, "But these are only kids." Who supported them? Why were they mature enough, many of them, to go back to school afterwards and pass matric? Those issues were not explored publicly, which is problematic because you have not endorsed the contribution of the entire community. You've left kids for many years afterwards thinking they, on their own, can make the world change.

'Not long ago, I listened to an exchange between two ten-year-old boys in Soweto. One said, "How can you burn an old man like this?" The other replied, "No, I didn't burn him. I burnt his arm, that's all." I listened to that and I felt very, very cold inside. Ten years from now, what will have become of that child who has no notion of respect for humanity?

'Why do we have kids like that? Partly because politicians have a way of playing on emotions: that's how they operate. They thrive on ignorance. They undermine existing social structures to facilitate their own agendas. It suited some politicians to have wild kids during the 1980s. It suited them to say, "No, never mind your parents, come with us."

'Now, if you're looking at a black family, you're looking at a very, very strong structure. Age is important; you cannot talk to certain people except in a regulated way. There are intricate networks which everyone must respect. That's what keeps the family together.

'Those families comprise the community, and the community will have the same kinds of structures. Now comes a political organisation, which begins to undermine existing structures. As soon as you do that and don't put anything in their place, you're in trouble, because what happens is that the children no longer gain strength from the family. They look elsewhere for support and find only politicians, who are busy manipulating their minds anyway. They're encouraged by politicians to hold on to a notion, a political ideology, which is never there for them personally. The intolerance of present-day politics teaches them to disrespect all other social systems. Take the political movement away, or let it discredit itself, and you've removed the only thing the child believes in. It's the only thing he believes will improve his life. And it's a lie.

'What the politicians who have done this are beginning to realise is that they are the ones who will ultimately have to sort out the problem. At least there's justice in that fact. They've created these delinquents and they will have to live with them. We in development will try to reconstruct, to create opportunities for these many thousands of young people. But we can't start that process until the politicians' game is over, after the election. The politicians still have an interest in manipulating certain groups, promising them everything to keep them aggressive and unhappy, until they've cast their votes.

'So where does the truth lie in all this mess, this crisis? You ask me and I'm asking you. It's a long, long story. And politics is a very, very cynical business.'

4

Nomsa's Marriage

T he windows of the Ford jalopy were steamed up from the heat of their passion. Neither Nomsa nor her lover saw the policeman as he approached, noting the car's registration number. It was only when Josiah heard the crackling of a radio that he sprang up from the back seat, accidentally shoving Nomsa's face against the door. She squealed with pain but held her breath when he spun around hissing, 'Shup!'

Wiping a small space on the fogged-up window, Josiah tried to decipher the shapes grouped in the darkness. It was raining but he could see a figure in the lighted cab of a vehicle parked behind and, he thought, other figures standing nearby. 'Police: kom's line,' (let's get out of here) he whispered urgently.

Struggling to fasten his trousers, Josiah yanked the door handle. Nomsa whimpered, 'Wait, my shoes,' but he was already out of the door. She stumbled blindly after him.

As the rain struck her face, Nomsa was aware of a flash of light from the police van. She could not see Josiah or hear anything above the clamour of her own fear. Running, grazing her arm against a branch, charging straight into a tree, she felt her head swelling with pain. A stone stabbed her foot but she raced on, propelled by terror, no sense in her mind beyond the compulsion to run.

* * *

That was the night Josiah Madumo decided to marry Nomsa Matlala. Huddled beside the dying fire in his aunt's kitchen in the early hours of Good Friday, 1973, a blanket tucked around him but unable to stop shivering, he thought longingly of Nomsa's warm body during the hours they had spent lovemaking in the back seat of the Ford. It was only at daybreak, when Josiah awoke feeling cramped and panicky, his sodden clothes lying in a heap on the floor, that he began to worry about Nomsa's safety.

He could barely remember his own journey home, bolting through rain, slipping in the mud. He and his friend Ben had drunk a lot of beer at Five Stars shebeen earlier in the evening. Nomsa, who did not touch liquor, had tugged at his arm several times, pleading to leave, but Ben was a forceful character.

It was Josiah's sixth date with Nomsa. He had strong feelings for her so he finally resisted Ben's entreaties and staggered out of the shebeen, his arm around her shoulders. Ben followed, but instead of arguing about their departure as expected, he offered them a car he had borrowed for the evening.

'I have no driver's licence,' protested Josiah.

'Don't worry, my bra. Take a ride. Take a ride.'

'Where did you get the car? Whose car is it?'

'Easy, man, Don't be a magu (idiot). You ask too many questions. Don't be a sissy boy all your life. If you want me to fix a job for you, you must not be a magu. Go!'

Nomsa hated Ben and she said so as they drove away. 'You two must be friends,' replied Josiah, placing his hand firmly on Nomsa's thigh and revving the engine.

* * *

Josiah dressed quietly and waited for the family to wake up. He had decided to send a messenger to Nomsa's parents later in the morning in order to start marriage negotiations. Would they accept him as a suitable husband for Nomsa, he pondered.

The answer came a few hours later, while Josiah was trying to persuade one of his cousins to act as a go-between. Nomsa's sister arrived, warning him to stay away for fear of her father's wrath following Nomsa's arrival home at dawn, carried on the back of a man who had found her lying exhausted at the side of a street after her flight from the police. Elias Matlala was baying for Josiah's blood, his daughter reported. 'I'll kill that boy if I see him,' the old man, a muscular former boxer, had declared.

A week passed. Josiah grew more and more tense waiting for news from Nomsa; he dared not approach her. However, Nomsa was Elias's favourite among his ten children, and she was clearly in love with Josiah. With quiet persistence, she eventually succeeded in convincing her father that Josiah was a decent boy.

'He is looking for djudju (honest work) and I will not want to marry him until he has a job,' Nomsa said.

'I will not allow you to marry an unemployed boy,' her father replied.

Three weeks after the Easter incident, Nomsa sent word to Josiah that her father had agreed to call a family meeting to decide whether or not the pair could marry. Josiah was overjoyed. But he had no job and he began to worry to the point of sleeplessness about the probability that her family would not accept him. 'They do not have to say no; they can just make the lobola (bride price) so high that I have no chance of paying it,' Josiah complained to Ben one night at Five Stars.

'These are urban people,' said Ben. 'They are not going to ask you for so many head of cattle that you can't pay. We live in modern times, man. Her father will accept a deposit and the rest in monthly instalments. Have another pint of divorce (beer).'

'But I do not have work.'

'Then you must take the job I offered you,' replied Ben with a triumphant smile.

* * *

The wedding was an elaborate affair. Pin-striped suits were hired for the groom and the best man. A seamstress in Jabavu fashioned Nomsa's gown from white tulle and lace. She wore a bridal head-dress known as a nuptial pillbox, with a veil of fine frothy fabric. Her bridesmaids wore turquoise satin. Nomsa's mother, a thin, brittle woman who was jealous of her eldest daughter's close relationship with Elias, told a neighbour confidentially that the bridal gown was worth all the money Elias had paid because it made Nomsa look pretty for the first time in her life.

The cake arrived in several boxes the day before the wedding. The man who delivered it had no idea how it was meant to be assembled. Nomsa's family — by now including relatives from several parts of the country, all crammed into the small house in Orlando — laid the complex pieces out on the kitchen table and argued about which icing sugar pillars belonged where. All they could agree on — until Nomsa's mother stepped in and insisted on deciding the matter — was that the tiny plastic bride and groom must stand at the top. The miniature model of a stork carrying a baby in a sling was included among the marriage symbols, they all agreed, only in case the cake was not eaten but kept until the christening of the first child. It should under no circumstances appear on the wedding cake, said Nomsa's mother, glancing knowingly at the bride.

The lounge of Elias's house was gaudy with balloons and ribbons cut from crêpe paper. One of the younger children had been appointed to hitch up the streamers when they came unstuck. It was not a job that suited a boy, he felt, and complained bitterly about the injustice. Elias had ordered a goat which he brought home in a wheelbarrow, legs bound with rags, mouth gagged, eyes staring in terror. He took the beast to the backyard and slaughtered it with one mighty lunge of a knife into its heart. When he entered the lounge, his dirty overalls were spattered with blood.

The younger children were so excited that two of them dressed up in their wedding garments hours before the event while their mother was at a neighbour's house helping to prepare massive pots of stew and relish. When she returned, she exploded with outrage at the sight of their grubby clothes.

The ceremony was held at the Methodist Church at 3 o'clock on a Saturday afternoon. Relatives and friends filed quietly into pews which were soon jammed with bodies. Latecomers had to stand at the back. Nomsa's aunt from the Transkei walked up the aisle asking those in the pews to share hymn sheets and pass the spare ones to unseated guests. A scuffle broke out in a row of children because some of them refused to relinquish their sheets. One child suffered a bleeding nose; a low murmur spread through the church as surrounding guests searched for handkerchiefs.

Josiah and Nomsa Madumo on their wedding day in Soweto twenty years ago.
Photograph: Victor Matom

Nomsa walked in on her father's arm, smiling with trembling lips. Josiah and Ben, his best man, came to the front of the church through another door. The priest was lighting a candle that had blown out. Josiah looked handsome in his grey suit, but nervous and awkward. It was Ben who shone at the altar, his white teeth gleaming in a broad grin beneath his glossy black moustache as he watched the bride's approach with frank admiration.

After the service, which brought tears to the eyes of most of the women in the congregation, Ben hurriedly signed the register and left for his other, more cherished role in the wedding proceedings. He had provided the bridal car, a streamlined white Chevrolet with messages written in lipstick on the back window. He had refused to reveal its ownership or history to Josiah.

Once Josiah and Nomsa, her voluminous skirt billowing half way up the window, were settled in the back of the Chev, Ben leapt into the driver's seat. With a mighty roar of the engine, he released the handbrake, waved gaily to the confetti-covered crowd and shot forward. The bridal couple's heads jolted alarmingly. The guests laughed and clapped.

At Elias's house, Nomsa stepped from the car on to a carpet of straw mats entwined with ivy. A photographer elbowed his way through the crowd and began clicking his camera. The bride and groom were guided to their places of honour and the speeches began, rumbling on for well over an hour. Then the party got underway.

It was a boisterous, happy celebration until drunkenness unleashed destructive potential among the guests. Loosening tongues, the alcohol found its first casualty: Elias. On hearing a rumour that a youngster called Zach had just raped his third daughter, the father of the bride thundered around the house, bellowing the youth's name. When Zach appeared, looking dishevelled, Elias lunged forward, striking vicious blows to the boy's head.

Josiah passed out around midnight. Nomsa tried to revive him with coffee, perfume in his nostrils and sharp pinches, but he slept on. When she attempted to dunk his head in a basin of water, his arm flew towards her face, striking her hard on the cheek. 'He didn't mean to hit you,' said one of the bridesmaids soothingly. But Nomsa was inconsolable. She lay on her bed sobbing until her eyes were swollen and her nose blocked. Then she fell asleep.

The drinking slowed down eventually. Most of the older guests went home. The lights in the lounge had been turned out while a few couples danced in writhing embraces. Elias's oldest son got into a fight over a girl and called for his father's help. Barely able to stand, Elias began to punch his son's assailant but sustained such a hard blow to the head when he slipped and hit a chair that he was left lying on the stoep, out cold for the remainder of the party.

Josiah woke up and went in search of Nomsa. Realising after an embarrassing embrace that the body in Nomsa's bed was one of her country aunts, he crawled around the house, peering at sleeping faces until he found his bride. They were busy making love when Nomsa's oldest brother crawled on to the mattress beside them and began to laugh uncontrollably.

Everyone agreed next morning that the wedding had been a great success. Stumbling about amid the chaos of bodies, empty bottles and fallen streamers, Josiah realised the rented suit he was still wearing had sustained serious damage during the revelry. Nomsa examined its ripped lapel and muddied knees, agreeing that they would have to pay for it.

Nomsa's mother eyed Josiah with unconcealed contempt. He was not the umkyenyana (son-in-law) she would have chosen for Nomsa: too weak and too poor, she thought. The traditional sacrificial ceremony, marking the bride's womanhood, was soon to be held at Elias's home. Another goat would be killed, its blood representing Nomsa's lost virginity. 'How many months left?' she asked Nomsa unkindly, appraising her daughter's stomach.

* * *

Nomsa and Josiah had no choice but to live at Elias's house after their marriage. Josiah's family had long ago disintegrated. His father had run off with a young woman and his mother, desperate to support five children, had turned to prostitution in the mining compounds surrounding Johannesburg.

Living in Elias's overcrowded house was not pleasant. Returning each day after working in a canning factory, Elias wallowed in self-pity, drinking cartons of sorghum beer and neat brandy. He complained constantly, in agitated bursts of cigarette smoke, about the bad-tempered white foreman under whom he worked, the school fees he had to pay, the noise of the children, the burden of a son-in-law whose part-time job unpacking crates in a supermarket provided little money.

Nomsa's mother quarrelled with everyone in the family and went about her daily chores with an air of aggrieved innocence. Nomsa played with her baby son and cooked. She took in washing, spending much of her time behind the colourful curtain of laundry that flapped on four lines of rope behind the house.

The years drifted by. After the birth of her second son, Nomsa became more aggressive. Her desire for a home of her own became an obsession. She railed at her husband but sobbed for long periods on her bed with a blanket over her head whenever her mother and father launched campaigns of criticism against Josiah. Elias loathed Josiah and barely spoke to him but never lost an opportunity to dash Nomsa's hopes of a brighter future on the grounds of her husband's worthlessness. Elias and his wife argued continually. Nomsa fought with her mother. The younger children, some of whom no longer attended school but had failed to find employment, also quarrelled bitterly with their mother.

Nomsa's misery eventually focused on her need for a lock-up cupboard in which to keep her family's clothing and belongings. She was a careful minder of their things and it infuriated her when her sisters borrowed skirts and blouses without asking, or when Josiah's shirts disappeared without trace. She would daily make a neat pile in the bedroom corner of the little garments worn by her boys, which a few hours later were strewn across the floor.

On his way back to the house late one afternoon, Josiah paused to watch a family loading their furniture into a truck. A sofa and several chairs, mattresses, blankets, pots and a bicycle were piled high in the back of the vehicle, which would not start. The engine choked and spluttered. A crank handle was produced but failed to engage the motor. Josiah helped them push the truck along the road, but to no avail. They pushed it back into the yard as darkness fell, deciding to offload the furniture and try again in the morning. Josiah hung around, helping and chatting, glad of an excuse to delay his return home. When he finally left, the family was indoors preparing the evening meal.

Closing the gate, Josiah noticed a wardrobe in the yard. Barely visible from the road, it was wedged in a space behind a lean-to washroom and a fence tangled with unruly creeper. He thought of Nomsa's pleas for a cupboard of her own, and a plan began to form in his mind.

Instead of going home, Josiah walked to Five Stars and drank alone for a long time. He had never stolen a thing but this seemed too good an opportunity to miss. If the family caught him, he could claim he was moving the cupboard to safety for them. The beer numbed his conscience. He walked slowly back to the dark, silent house. The street was empty. He opened the gate and listened. Walking to the wardrobe, groping in the darkness, he ripped away at the foliage until he was able to grip the cupboard and drag it from behind the shed. Its door swung open with a sharp creak. Josiah held his breath but no sounds followed. His hands explored the base of the wardrobe: cracked sections of chipboard rested on a narrow ledge. A few were nailed but most came away easily. Edging his way through the door into the wardrobe, Josiah flattened his hands against the wooden roof, spread his feet sideways, lifted the cupboard above his head and cautiously stepped forward. It worked: the top of the cupboard was secure. He moved towards the gate.

Near Nomsa's parents' house, a scream shattered the stillness. Shouting followed. A dog began to howl. Josiah considered opening the door and bolting but his legs moved faster, automatically. He had to keep the cupboard tilted slightly backward so that the door would remain shut. He tripped several times but managed to restore his balance. His arms began to shake uncontrollably. Not knowing if he could stay on the road without stopping to peer through the door, he stumbled blindly onward.

His journey ended abruptly when several bodies stepped in front of the wardrobe. The door swung open. Fists and hands fell on Josiah, dragging him out. He recognised the woman screaming: an old crone in the neighbourhood whose life's mission was to warn of the vengeance of witchcraft. 'It is the cupboard that walks,' she was yelling hysterically. 'I have seen the cupboard that walks.'

'It's a thief, mama,' said a man whose thick arms were clasped around Josiah's neck.

Sounds of a vehicle and the sudden illumination of headlights silenced the huddle. A door slammed; a voice boomed authoritatively. It was a policeman, routinely patrolling the streets. Josiah was punched and pushed into the back of the van, where he lay in the foetal position, wishing he were dead.

He was warned and again beaten at the police station. Eventually released, he staggered home and crept under the blanket beside Nomsa shortly before dawn. The old woman rushed from house to house next morning telling her story about the walking wardrobe. Josiah waited for his crime to be revealed to Nomsa and her parents. But luck was at last on his side: the neighbourhood discussed versions of the event all day but his name was never mentioned.

Josiah began to drink very heavily in the months that followed. Every evening he met Ben at Five Stars, returning late at night after Nomsa and her family were asleep. 'I know why they call Bantu beer divorce,' Nomsa told Josiah one morning. 'Maybe it is time for you to leave your wife and children.'

The next evening Josiah met Ben at the shebeen as usual, but he returned home early in a jaunty mood. 'Now I have a job which will bring plenty of money,' he announced as the pap was being dished out in the kitchen. Elias grunted scornfully. Seeing Josiah's guarded expression when she asked him what work he would be doing, Nomsa realised her husband had accepted one of Ben's crooked deals. But she no longer cared about legality.

The money was immediately apparent. Josiah bought himself new clothes, toys for the children, a new outfit for Nomsa. Then he arrived with news that reduced Nomsa to helpless giggles of joy: he had found a two-roomed shack, leak-proof and private. Situated in the backyard of another house, it was at least a home of their own.

Two years later they moved into a proper house on its own plot, though Nomsa had been told only a few days earlier by the clerk at the Superintendent's Office that the waiting list for houses remained miles long. Ben had somehow managed to acquire it. But having given his help, Ben began to treat their home as his own. He was always there, boasting and flirting with Nomsa. She despised him, making no secret of her feelings. But she was powerless to get rid of him. 'Why doesn't he marry and have children of his own?' Nomsa asked Josiah, who shrugged helplessly.

When Ben was not around, Nomsa was happy in her small, neat home. She no longer took in washing; Josiah made enough money to meet all the family's needs. Initially, she implored her husband to tell her how he acquired his money, but Josiah was determined to keep what was clearly a dangerous secret. He still drank a lot and he worked mostly at night, sleeping for long periods during the day, but he was kind to her and the children, and generous with his money. Nomsa was content.

* * *

Although he kept odd hours, Josiah was invariably home in bed by dawn. One cold morning in May, however, Nomsa woke to find his side of the mattress empty. Fear clutched her throat. There was no way of knowing where he might be. She sent the children to school and tried to concentrate on the housework while waiting for Ben to arrive at lunchtime, as usual. 'Where is he?' she demanded, opening the door as she saw Ben walking up the path.

'Who?'

'Josiah. He didn't come home.'

Ben returned hurriedly to his car and drove off in a cloud of dust. Neither he nor Josiah came back. Nomsa hovered all day beside the front window, looking down the street and praying.

Early next morning, Nomsa decided to check the hospital. Taking a taxi to Baragwanath, she queued for a long time until a clerk finally appeared at the barred window in front of her. 'Yes?' He searched the admissions records, stopping to drink a cup of tea and chew ponderously on a sandwich. Nomsa wanted to scream but controlled herself. She thought of telling her story to an older woman who was also waiting anxiously to learn the fate of a missing relative but reconsidered for fear of having to formulate in words the terrible question that was crouching in her mind: was Josiah dead?

At three in the afternoon, the clerk called an orderly, telling him to show Nomsa to the mortuary. 'Sorry, ma,' he said through the bars. 'I think you might find your husband there.'

The mortuary was far away, up and down corridors and the many pathways that stretch alongside Baragwanath's barrack-like wards. Following the attendant into a room that seemed to contain hundreds of large grey filing cabinets, she was ushered forward by a man in a white coat. He pulled open a drawer and pointed to the face of the body which lay in it. Josiah stared back at her. He was naked, a small wound gaping above his heart.

Ben drove Nomsa to the funeral. She watched her sons throw clods of earth on to their father's coffin, shaking Ben's arm from her shoulders. Why had Josiah died? Who had killed him? She would never know the answers. Except that Ben was to blame.

Driving home afterwards, Ben told her: 'You must decide about the house. Widows are not allowed to rent houses in Soweto; you know that.'

'I'll talk about it later,' said Nomsa.

They drove in silence. One of the children in the back seat leant forward and asked: 'Will we lose the house, mama?'

When Nomsa did not answer, Ben replied: 'You will lose it unless your mother marries me.'

5

Red Alert

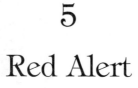

T he social pathology of Soweto is dramatically reflected in
the case histories of patients at Baragwanath, known as
Bara, a 3 400-bed hospital which ranks among the largest in the
world. Particularly telling is Bara's casualty section, known as
The Pit, an enormous room in which the brutally assaulted
victims of Soweto's violent society are treated in droves every
weekend.

Given Ngema, a handsome young man known as Gavin, is a
paramedic in the ambulance unit serving Bara. With his
colleague and friend, Lybon Makhubele, known as Al, he has
been rescuing the sick and injured of Soweto for the past ten
years. They are figures of considerable status in the community, having conducted a campaign to ensure that ambulances
are no longer attacked during times of rioting in the township.
Better qualified than anyone else to monitor current levels of
violence in Soweto, both Al and Gavin say it is much higher
than newspaper reports indicate. 'I don't read the papers any
more,' says Gavin. 'Those reports are very superficial.'

They are familiar with every street in Soweto's vast and
incomprehensible maze. They understand the political land-

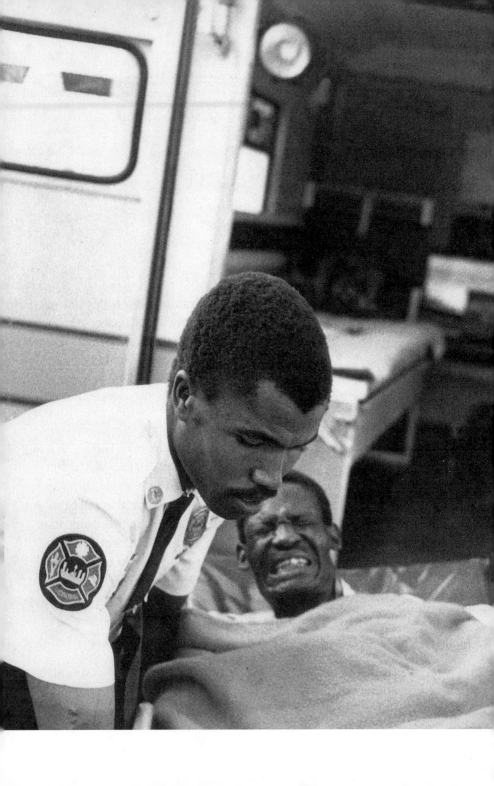

Courageous paramedics Gavin Ngema (left) and Al Makhubele are well qualified to monitor levels of violence in Soweto.
Photograph: Victor Matom

scape so well that they can predict accurately which groups will be involved simply from a radio location report of an outbreak of violence. They frequently arrive at the scene of a clash as the attackers are still wielding axes, firearms, grenades, knives or pangas. Sometimes people are killed as Gavin and Al watch helplessly from the relative safety of their ambulance.

Theirs is a dangerous and depressing job, says Al, an engaging character with a gravelly voice. To maintain a tolerable environment for themselves, the two have developed a comic routine: after safely off-loading their patients at Bara, they conduct a swift frolic among the nurses on duty in The Pit. Pinching bottoms and kissing cheeks in a brief razzle of hilarity on the way back to the ambulance, Gavin and Al return to their sombre duties in the streets of Soweto.

Gavin explains that he is going to trace the genesis of Soweto's political violence for us. We drive in an Emergency Services vehicle to a place called Tladi Camp. 'It is just shacks and some houses bombed by grenades. I got a call late one night in 1990 when I was driving in a response car. I came. It was dark. You see two high masts of light over there; that one wasn't functioning. The other was also faulty. It would come on for about a minute and then switch off. I got out of the car. There was crying from injured people. The light switched off, and when it went, machine gun firing started. I only realised that when I was already in and there was no way out for me. I had casualties next to me, I had to treat and I had to transport. And there was gunfire. Every time the light went off, firing. Most unfortunately, the police were around in their cars when I arrived, but they were the first to go. I was left alone.

'So I carried on. In this demolished house there was a male in his late twenties, who was shot with his baby in his arms. A bullet grazed the child's hand and went into the father. He died, still holding the baby. I took the baby from the father's arms. I asked neighbours, where was the mother? They said she split from the father; only the two of them were in that house that night. I put the child in the car.

'The light was coming on, going off. I stabilised, stopped most of the bleeding, put drips on six casualties, hoping the ambulances would follow. There were five dead; nothing I could do for them. But the ambulances didn't come. So I loaded all five with the baby, the blood and all the likes in the response car, and moved off because there was still gunfire.'

We are standing in Tladi Camp at the place where Gavin parked his response car that night. 'It was believed here by the residents that they were being attacked by people living at Merafe Hostel, which is nearby,' explains Gavin. 'Now, the story of the hostels in Soweto: there are twelve of them with around four thousand people in each. They are 95 per cent Zulu dominated and the other 5 per cent go along with Zulu demands. The Zulus in this country, most of them support Mangosuthu Buthelezi, the leader of the Inkatha Freedom Party (IFP). What happened is that everybody who wasn't a Zulu in the hostels was chucked out by the Zulus when this political violence started at the end of 1989. So the hostels are very much Zulu strongholds. The rest of Soweto, the township residents, support the African National Congress (ANC). Nelson Mandela is their hero.

'So these people at Tladi Camp believed they were attacked by Merafe Hostel. But I knew that was not true because on the way here, responding to the call, I came past Merafe. The hostel was all quiet. Everybody was asleep there, late at night. It was a completely wrong impression on the part of the township residents. When I arrived, they said those Zulus from Merafe were attacking them and I couldn't argue, otherwise you are seen as taking sides. But it was very much clear in my mind that these people at Tladi were not attacked by Merafe residents.

'I have seen the hostels, Merafe and all the others, when they are ready for attacks; when some of them are already in the township attacking, and those left to guard the hostel are in fighting mood. They don't sleep. Throughout the night they stay outside with their weapons, walk around, make a noise, sing war songs; nobody sleeps.

'That night, it was all quiet at Merafe. Even after I off-loaded the casualties at Bara I went to Merafe to check. It was quiet; everybody asleep. It was the first time a bell was ringing in my mind. Somebody else launched that attack on Tladi. The residents believed it was hostel dwellers, but it was not.'

We get back into the white Emergency Services car with ambulance insignia painted on its doors. Gavin was recently promoted to a senior position, controlling the paramedics in the region, and he virtually lives in the vehicle. Parked outside his Soweto home every night, it is seldom stationary for longer than an hour or two. He sleeps with a shortwave radio beside his bed, responding to the calls which might require his supervision.

'From here, I will show you Naledi Zone 2, where I responded to the same political violence, later the same night.' We drive along dirt roads that are muddy from recent rain. It is November 1993, four years since black political rivalry unleashed yet another bleak chapter into South Africa's bloodstained history. A black and red cockerel wanders across our path, with green and yellow ribbons hanging from its neck. They are the colours of the ANC, black, green, gold — and unmistakably so; a rallying symbol for millions of black South Africans, a warning to their opponents. Gavin stops the car, waiting for the creature to pass. A man tending his garden in a house alongside tells us the rooster wants to be knocked down. 'It's waiting to go to a better life,' he says. 'The wish will be granted,' retorts Gavin, 'because somebody will eat it before long.'

Ahead of us is a bridge. 'You see these tunnels under the railway line? At night it's very, very dark; nothing you can see from there or into those tunnels. No street lights, nothing. I came in an ambulance with Al for that call. I don't remember which house it was here; that one, yes. One hundred metres from the bridge.'

Gavin parks the car. 'It was a B1-plus-plus call, a very urgent, critical case,' says Al, adjusting his Ray-Bans.

'When we arrived the people here were also complaining they were being attacked by IFP,' says Gavin. 'I spoke my mind that time, which as paramedics we shouldn't do. One of the patients, a lady about sixty years of age, was crying about Zulus. I listened to get her side of the story; who was attacking? Then I said, "No, I don't believe it." She said, "What!" — very much surprised. I repeated, and told her my story. When I came here, I went past Merafe Hostel and everybody was asleep. She was thinking. Then she said, "No, you could be right." I said, "Why?" And she told me she remembered now that the people who were attacking were black, but pitch black: very, very dark. And the accent they were talking with wasn't from Zulus. They were talking Zulu but with another accent. When they shouted their war-cry, Usuthu, you could hear from the word that this is a Zulu. But the accent wasn't Zulu.

'That was the first person to confirm my suspicions. She said, "Yes, you can be right. They didn't talk any of our languages, either Tsonga, Xhosa, Sotho, even Zulu; only some few words of war-cry and songs they learnt, maybe in one day.

It just had to be black faces doing the attacking." When you hear there are black, black faces, you think of northern Africa. And your suspicion is that they are hired killers.

'Then, whilst we were busy treating, right from those three tunnels came machine gun fire, so close. We reversed the ambulances — three of them, I don't remember how many casualties that time — and carried on treating the patients as we were retreating.'

Returning the way we had come, we stop in front of another house in the same street. 'I got another call here, the same night again, or maybe early in the morning. Still very, very dark. A 74-year-old male. His wife was also old. The man was dead; the lady still alive. The neighbours said it is a political killing: IFP. I did not argue but I was thinking, who said they were active ANC, this old man and his old wife? If I was an IFP warrior hitting one house by itself, I would hit activists, people who are active in politics, not people who will be dying soon naturally in any case from old age, tomorrow, maybe even before they can vote.

'We had four houses hit that night, this one here, another in the next street. The residents did not ask, "Why do you have a two-year-old shot here, a 70-year-old shot there, and an 18-year-old, all because they're ANC supporters. What does a two-year-old know about politics?" One of the houses that was hit had Zulus living inside. There are many Zulus living among the residents of Soweto. The IFP wants those people to support Buthelezi. They can't vote if they are dead.

'In 1991, the newspapers started saying it is the third force doing the political killing. We knew it already then, that night. The basis is third force. The attacks are instigated by the third force. After it starts, yes, then the residents and the hostel dwellers are the ones doing the fighting but they don't start it right at the beginning. All the attacks are being perceived by both organisations as counter-attacks.

'The third force, I believe, is right-wing radical whites. It's not necessarily the police, as many residents believe, except maybe some dark units of the police or army. It's organised crime, I'm sure; organised by specialist killer squads. Each time they struck, no one was caught. Still they haven't been caught, up to this day, after many, many train massacres when people are just sitting innocently in a train and masked gunmen suddenly come in and shoot them or beat them to death. Why have they never been caught? After so many killings in the township, which have been happening nearly every day for years now, why are the culprits not caught?

'They are not caught because they are professional killers, and very good at it. They do it to cause chaos politically. They want to show the world, and white people here, that blacks are not ready to vote. You cannot invest in South Africa because it is not a stable country. You cannot give political power to blacks because they cannot even live with each other. How can you trust these people to run the country?'

We are talking in the stationary vehicle, a short distance from the railway bridge. 'Now, on the very same night again, I responded to one victim of assault, also here in Naledi. The man who was attacked stayed in Merafe Hostel. And most unfortunately for him, he was Xhosa. The other inmates, Zulus, kicked him out. In actual fact, they wanted to kill him. They assaulted him all over, told him he was Mandela's follower and everything else. When I arrived, they had chased him here. There were assegais, spears, sticks, and they wanted to finish him off.

'I don't know what gave me the bravery to approach them and ask them to pardon him for his life, because I could be another victim myself. But still, I went and had a word with them; told them now they've finished him, he can't fight back, nothing you can do with him. Zulus believe in heroism, and their heroism is not based on attacking somebody who cannot fight back. It is based on having a fight with an opponent who can win. So I told them, "No, he's finished. He can't fight back." They would be cowards to finish him off when he's already down. And they left.

'We loaded him in the ambulance, a very critical case. And now, the local residents were all in the street. We put on sirens, lights and drove. But the residents knew that man was from the hostel and anybody, according to them, who's from the hostel must be IFP. And they also wanted to take him and finish him off. They stopped the ambulance. They were Sotho people. I had to convince them that this man is not an IFP supporter. He's been attacked by the IFP. They said, no, he's got scars on his face (ritual tribal scarifications); he's a Zulu because of the marks. Those Sotho have difficulty differentiating between Zulu and Xhosa: they are very close, even the language.

'I managed to persuade them, with difficulty. They opened the ambulance and were trying to get him. It was a crowd and they were hungry to get him. He was an unwanted one, both sides. After what they perceived as being IFP attacks that night, so many people killed, they wanted him dead. But they let the ambulance pass and he survived.

'It took not so much bravery, but a miracle. That man had to survive. It wasn't time for him, and he did survive, against all odds.'

Al says: 'Many of the victims who have died from political violence since 1990 were those Zulus who show their culture or beliefs. When they slaughter goats, they make bracelets from the skin to wear on the arms. Only Zulus do that. Those bracelets make you a victim to the township residents. They'll kill you if you wear one, if there has been killing which they think was done by the hostel dwellers. Many Zulus have stayed within the community here for many, many years, but if they wear that bracelet at the wrong time, they are dead. You can't wear those things from Zulu culture in Soweto, even the big open ears or marks on the face, which they had to have for the custom, even if they didn't want it. They have it there, on their faces, on their ears, and they cannot take it away because it is there. Now they must die for it.'

Gavin: 'This situation came only since the political violence began. Before then you could be a Zulu in Soweto: it was OK, with whatever things on your face and ears and arms. The ANC's first president was a Zulu. Albert Luthuli, another ANC president, was also a Zulu.'

Al: 'Township residents, Xhosas, Sothos, used to go and wash inside the hostels because there were showers and many did not have showers in their houses. They could go in, come out, no problem. Hostel dwellers could walk around the township, buy some things, have your hair cut, walk around, house to house, door to door, no problem. But now ...'

The radio in Gavin's car hisses with continual location reports to the seven ambulances that serve Soweto throughout each day and night. An urgent call is being relayed, B1-plus-plus. Gavin puts his foot down; Al switches on the emergency lights and turns the dial of the siren. We race into the middle of the narrow road, pedestrians scurrying out of the way, cars weaving uncertainly. Anxious eyes follow the screaming, dazzling vehicle; a small child puts his hands over his ears.

It is a medical case; an elderly, frightened man, close to death. Gavin and Al resuscitate him: oxygen, drip, urgency. An ambulance arrives. Two paramedics push a stretcher through the crowd that has swelled outside the house.

* * *

'This is Chicken Farm,' says Gavin as we drive into a settlement of utter squalor. 'No lights at night, just candles there and there. The reason I bring you here is to show the conditions under which so many people live in Soweto. Then you can understand why we have such high domestic violence. This area used to have chicken runs. Now they are human runs, meant for chickens, not for people.

'In each of these shacks — you can see the biggest is four square metres — a whole family lives. I call it a five-in-one: bedroom, bathroom, kitchen, dining room, lounge, all in one room, and maybe ten people living there, in each one. I started in one of these myself, before I got enough money to build a house.

'You have no control. You may be living next door to people who don't want to be clean. They leave all their dirt outside. Others, you can see, are very, very clean. That woman is sweeping outside. She has grown some flowers. She wants to live nicely. But it is psychologically frustrating to live here. You can sweep all day and throughout the night but still you cannot make it clean if the neighbour is dirty. You cannot be alone, not for one minute. Irrespective of the ages, all must sleep together, from babies to old men. You don't have anything that is yours. I think it is sometimes why people steal. They have nothing so they don't understand how it feels to have something that is taken away. They just take it.'

We drive around Chicken Farm, tyres squelching on make-shift roads that are running with rain water and sewage. Of twenty-two million blacks living in South Africa's urban areas, the Urban Foundation estimates that four million have access only to minimal, untreated water. Seven million have minimal sanitation facilities. About 90 per cent do not have domestic electricity.

'We've had many casualties here from fire, where up to ten shacks burn down at once because of one candle falling; because of the way the shacks are crowded. Burn cases come a lot from areas like this, especially in winter when people try to keep warm from the flames of fires in the yard. Check on this side: they have built shacks in the valley below the flood line. If we should get very heavy rains, a lot of shacks and people will be washed away.

'The ones who stay here include immigrants, those from rural areas, those who have had to flee their homes after political violence, or those who are on waiting lists for rented houses. If you are on a waiting list, you can stay there for life; you are waiting for the grave. Children grow up, they get married in Chicken Farm, they stay with their parents in these shacks and have their own children. Your whole life is spent in one room.

'Now I will take you to see an area where people had to flee their homes and come to Chicken Farm because of political violence.' Gavin is referring to the lower middle-class families who have been forced to abandon their homes in established residential areas because they were situated near hostels. In repeated attacks by hostel dwellers, many houses have been destroyed or rendered too dangerous for habitation. Their occupants are often left with no option but to move into squatter camps from houses and gardens they have carefully tended for years.

'On the way there we are driving through Dlamini. And here I can tell you about the rent boycott, which started ten years ago. The residents of Soweto have not paid rent for ten years. They say it is ending this month, but we will see.

'We are passing municipal houses which people rented. They were paying their rent every month up to 1983. Now, as they understood the renting of houses, they expected the municipality to do the maintenance on the houses, to fix the streets, provide electricity and services, which they were promised. But now, since people stayed in these houses for long, paying rent, without the municipality renovating them or providing normal maintenance, the people decided they will stop paying rent and use that money to fix up the houses themselves. They'd had enough. That's how the rent boycott started. You can see there are many houses here, freshly painted, extensions added. This was going on long before the government announced recently that people who have rented houses for a long time can take ownership.

'You can see from this that it is untrue, as many whites believe, that black people don't care how they live. The rent boycott was a good thing for Soweto, otherwise all these houses would be dilapidated. But they are not; some are, but most look all right. And all of them are very clean inside. That tells any normal thinking human being that the people of Soweto want to lead a good, clean life.'

We pass what Al calls a 'thug funeral' in Moroka: a hearse followed by several cars crammed with teenagers, some sitting on the roofs and bonnets. Their bodies are stretched out of the windows, fists in the air, screaming incoherent slogans.

'That thuggery is what is causing most of the domestic violence and crime in Soweto,' says Al. 'To be recognised as an important person when you are buried, you've got to behave in such a manner. What they are saying is, "Even those of us who never went to school, we can harass you if we want to."

That is harassment they are doing on the road. Everybody must get out of the way otherwise they can run you over, even shoot you from the car window. Even at the graveyard, the cultural meaning has been lost. These thugs don't have respect for the dead. They don't respect the grave. They shoot guns, right into the coffin sometimes. They spin their cars around the cemetery, make a lot of noise, smoke dagga.'

Gavin: 'Basically people want recognition and these days it doesn't matter what form of recognition. They want other people to recognise they exist. They'll do anything to get noticed. If you haven't gone to school, you haven't got a house, you haven't got a car. Whether you've gone past that way or that way, nobody notices. So if I am a thug, I steal a beautiful looking car so that when I pass people notice me. And I must drive it in such a way that people look and see it is me in that car. And, above that, I must have some form of authority. When I arrive in a place, people must know — I'm there. They must feel I'm there. So I carry a gun, hidden, but I take it out so they can see it. Or a knife. I sharpen it so others can see I have power, authority. They must speak respectfully to me. All this is because I have an inferiority complex which I'm trying to work against.

'The rape cases in Soweto — there are many and rising all the time — are caused by this thuggery. It is not the ones who are ugly and can't get girlfriends. It is not because they can't get consenting sex. They do have girlfriends. But still they go that extra mile, raping, often gang rapes, so that people can see they have authority.'

* * *

More than half the rape victims in Soweto are under sixteen years old. About 10 per cent of these are girls aged between one and five, according to statistics recently released by the

Soweto Medical Legal Unit at Baragwanath Hospital. Sixty per cent of all rape patients treated at Bara are victims of gang rape. One in four women in South Africa will be raped in her lifetime, according to statistics calculated by the National Institute for Crime Prevention and Rehabilitation of Offenders.

About half of all the legal abortions performed each month at Bara are on girls under the age of sixteen who have become pregnant due to rape, says district surgeon Dr Thamsanqa Bomvana. 'If one extrapolates the figures of the number of rapes reported, one could estimate that about two thousand rapes are committed each month in Soweto, most of which go unreported.'

Of great concern at Bara is the inevitability of some rape victims contracting the deadly HIV virus. 'The problem is that it costs about R80 to conduct one Aids test, and a possible victim may have to be tested up to three times. At the current rate, it could cost more than R32 000 a month to test the rape victims and we just don't have the money,' says Dr Bomvana. So most victims go untested unless they pay for it themselves.

* * *

'Basically, what's happened began in 1976, at the time of the students' uprising, when the black children decided they are going to take the lead to save their country, or to save their kind,' says Gavin. 'The black adults were more content then. As long as they earned a salary and they could feed their children, they were quiet. But their children did not see it that way. It was most frustrating for the black children, who were getting educated up until 1976, to see other white children prospering in life and doing all things they couldn't do. So they decided, this is it, we are no longer going to listen to our parents. We are going to take things in our own hands.

'The approach the children took in 1976 was an incorrect one. They were right to turn against the system, but not against their parents. They still needed guidance. If the parents don't give it, somebody else will. Those children came under the influence of criminals and politicians. They were used by both.

'Now, the very people who were students in 1976 are the parents of the young children today, who are not yet thugs. It is up to them to sort it out. It is too late for the ones who are already thugs, but it's up to the parents now to make sure it doesn't happen to the younger children.'

Says Al: 'I have already started right now with my kids. They are small but I motivate them by the way I look, the person I am. They start liking me and what I am doing. You can see them looking at others, saying I don't like that guy to be my father. But this one, a paramedic helping people, yes, I want to be like him. I'm monitoring my children; they're monitoring me. I know I must not do wrong things because the mistakes I make, they will follow. Same for the children of thugs; they will be thugs too. You must be a good role model. That's the best you can do to change all this thuggery. It is my job that makes me try harder to show young people they don't have to be thugs. This job has highlighted life at an advanced angle for me. I know what is important.'

Gavin: 'I was shocked one day recently to go home and find my own kids, little ones, playing "Kill the Boer, kill the farmer" just after that slogan was banned. They were singing. It was fun. Everybody in Soweto seems to be politicised, but not really.

'The people who stay in the township, ordinary people not politicians, 80 per cent of them are politically illiterate. That means — whether tomorrow it's Buthelezi as president, or

Nelson Mandela, or De Klerk — they don't care. They just want to carry on with life. What happened yesterday — the proceedings in negotiations, the elections and all that — they just don't care. All they want is to live, get a job, have a house, feed their children; that's it. Politicians, and journalists too, want to make it look like every person is a political philosopher. But it's not true.

'Over the last four years since the beginning of political violence, domestic violence has gone down. People have found something to do with their frustration. It's politics in a way for them, but again, not really. They're organising themselves into forces against evil forces, and that has brought them together in every street. They aren't fighting so much with each other. What also happened was those organised resident groups were policing around their streets. So if anybody was troublesome, they'd go for him. And so domestic crime was reduced.

'Ninety-nine per cent of domestic violence is drink related; 99.9 per cent in actual fact. And dagga. The old ones drink, the young ones take drugs. We're passing through Emdeni now, known as Beirut because of political violence, but the domestic violence here is worse. What I can say about alcohol is that people abuse it in Soweto. Frustration, family quarrels, unemployment, all that causes domestic violence, but the main generator is alcohol. All the trauma cases we attend to — motor vehicle accidents, assaults, murders — there's liquor inside the patients. It's rare to find two sober-minded people fighting in Soweto, very, very rare. I have never seen it. It's always one is drunk, one is sober, or they're both drunk.

'People are under the belief that if you have problems, you drink them over. But most unfortunately, the more you drink, the more problems you get. Until people understand that liquor is not a solution to problems, domestic violence will go on.

'We're passing through Zola now. It's rare to get political violence here, simply because there's no hostels. There are not many telephones in these houses. It is a problem we are having all over Soweto: ambulances take a long time getting to the scene. Unless somebody tells us, we don't know. People just expect to find an ambulance there, without taking the initiative of calling for one.

'That is the situation causing the perception that paramedics are taking sides. The hostel dwellers see us with sirens and lights responding to emergencies in the township. Residents see us with sirens and lights responding to violence in the hostels. But then, when residents are at the scene waiting for an ambulance which is late because nobody called us, that tells them we drive fast to hostels but not to them. Too many wrong perceptions; too many. It is very frustrating for us because in our profession we don't know colour, creed, culture, political affiliation. All we know is a patient. But they don't want to believe it. They never hear your words.

'You see, people lack trust. That's where the biggest problem is today. If you come and tell them that the real situation is this, they see you making cover-ups because of whatever faults or mishaps you did before, because of the colour of your skin, or the marks on your face.

'It has a lot to do with our background. Black people believe they've been robbed of their country and their belongings by the whites. And a Bible was used to rob them. The way the Bible was brought to them was as a book which had everything positive for them. Things would go right for them once they trusted God, once they prayed and all that, and once they lost all the wrong things they did. But instead they lost their country. They trusted the Bible and they stopped attacking people. They believed that if somebody does you wrong, you don't have to do it back. And since they adopted that stance they've lost so much. Now it is difficult to trust anybody who comes with anything. You actually are guilty until you're proven innocent. Black people in South Africa are always afraid of hidden agendas.

'Most of my colleagues believe there is still apartheid within the ambulance service. They believe that, no matter what they can do, no matter what their qualifications, they get nowhere simply because they are black. I told these people, "You have been so abused by the white man's system over the past that, even if you get positive things coming your way, you are not ready to take them; you are not positive to meet them." All they see from whites is denying and attacking. That's where our mistrust stems from, and I don't see it ending tomorrow.

'Now, here we are in Meadowlands, at the hostel which is known as Sputnik. You see this hostel, all the broken windows, and the roof blown away, no doors; this is the result of attacks by Soweto residents living on the other side of the road. There are bullet marks on the walls, too many. Now we go to the other side of the road to the residents' houses: same thing. This house, a pile of rubble: it was bombed with grenades. This was counter-attack. But also the damage caused to the hostel was counter-attack. Houses were set alight, you can see, burnt down. Corrugated iron across the windows where the residents tried to hide from bullets and assegais. But they couldn't hide: they had to flee. Nobody can rebuild and live in these houses. They will die, as many before them have died here, in these houses. So the people who used to live here had to go to Chicken Farm. That is why I brought you here from Chicken Farm: one is a slum, one used to be a nice area. Now they are related through politics.'

We drive slowly past the wreckage of the ghost town in Meadowlands. 'Peace is Deaf', says a slogan on a wall. As we turn into Vincent 'Death' Road, a bizarre drama unfolds. A young white policeman springs into the street from behind a hedge, pistol pointing from his outstretched arm, charging towards a group of youths. His face is tensely drawn, sweating, terrifying and terrified.

Gavin steers to the other side of the road as we pass the white man. Our car drives on; Gavin's conversation doesn't pause. He seems scarcely to have noticed this lone white policeman, running, with his gun aimed. The scene from the rear window is one of sheer courage: the policeman is frisking the youths. His gun is still held in a taut arm, but he is piteously vulnerable.

* * *

One hundred and fifty men — mostly whites — make up the Soweto Flying Squad with responsibility for policing the most violent city on earth. Their average age is twenty-two years. Most have never entered a township before and are unable to speak a black language.

They are flung into Soweto with six months' preparatory training, the quality of which was illustrated in a documentary shown to British television viewers by Channel 4.

'Right, everybody!' shouts the training officer at a shooting range. 'The reason why you have to look first is that you have to identify if the person you are going to shoot at is the guy who shot at you, or if it is an innocent bystander. You must look if it is necessary for you to shoot ...'

Interrogation techniques are equally crude. Confronting a suspect, who is eventually, inexplicably judged by Flying Squad officers to have broken both his opponent's arms while 'boxing', the questioning goes like this:

Policeman: 'OK, you'd better start talking the truth, hey!'

Suspect: 'Excuse me, master?'

Policeman: 'I want the truth now. With what did you hit that man?'

Second Policeman: 'English! English!'

Suspect: 'I hit him with a ...'

Policeman: 'No, no, don't speak shit.'

Another sequence reveals a policeman's capacity for self-deception: 'We only wounded him,' he says, describing how he shot a car thief. 'But he died because of his wounds.'

Constable Rooies de Beer tells viewers that one of the joys of working in Soweto is that 'you are allowed to do things here you won't normally get to do in a white area.' Whites, he says, think they know their rights. 'The black people, they still have respect, if I can put it in that way.'

A sergeant gives the camera a guided tour of his home. 'This is like a normal area,' he declares. 'It's a lot different from Soweto.' He proudly points out a double set of iron gates that guard the entrance, an iron gate protecting the front door, iron bars covering the windows, the section of the house where his wife imprisons herself, with a pistol, Rottweiler and Pit-bull terrier, while he is on duty in Soweto.

Viewers were also given a clear view of the courage of the Soweto Flying Squad, many of whom have seen colleagues being killed. 'You don't know what to feel,' says one officer, recalling his emotions when two friends were shot dead on patrol. 'Confused,' cuts in another. 'Because you are trying to help the people and they are trying to kill you.'

6

Saturday

▼▼▼

J immy Ntintili's distinctive style does not match the subtle ambience in the plush mahogany lobby of Johannesburg's smartest hotel. Wearing jeans, sneakers and an air of authority, he issues brisk instructions to an obsequious doorman clad in top hat and tails, then smacks him reassuringly on the shoulder.

Both men live in Soweto and enter the hushed precincts of the Carlton Hotel daily in order to serve the world's roving rich. The doorman, like most blacks who cross the marble foyer, is an anonymous servant. Jimmy is something else. He negotiated with the hotel's management a few years ago for permission to ply his trade as a tour operator and then took the matter a bold step beyond the norms of South African race relations: he gave himself permission to be himself.

'I'm not glossy,' he says. 'There's nothing wrong with it but I prefer the way I am. If you have to be what others think you should be — a black man, a servant, lucky to walk in a place like this, fortunate to talk to wealthy people — you will be a dull boy and nothing more. I take people as they come to me, as people, never mind the cameras, the white skin, and the big bags of money.'

'Welcome to Jimmy's Face to Face Tours,' he declares, grinning broadly at a group of tourists who have booked to visit Soweto with him. 'My Soweto includes everything up to the year 2000. I'm talking Soweto yesterday, today and tomorrow.'

We board one of Jimmy's minibuses, fill up with petrol, and head for the Soweto highway. He is telling a complicated story in an agitated, passionate voice, much to the bemusement of his passengers. A friend, who lives near him in Soweto, was raped at her home a week earlier while Jimmy was in Germany promoting his tours. The intruders stole a vehicle. But that is not the point, bellows Jimmy. The point is that the police in Soweto are treating the crime as two separate incidents, and they are more concerned about the theft than the rape. 'The sergeant says to me, "Oh, the rape. I do not know about that. It is a matter for another department." He didn't know if he was going or coming when I asked about the rape.

'Rape is a common event in Soweto. Even the police can dismiss it, believe me or not. "Oh, the rape. I do not know about that",' Jimmy mimics. His eyes bulge in an exaggerated show of the sergeant's surprise. We watch his distress through his rear-view mirror until the story is told and his mood changes. 'That's enough moaning,' he announces jauntily as the little brick houses and shacks of Soweto appear ahead, stretching forth in long rows as far as the eye can see.

The oldest township in Soweto is Orlando East, established in 1930. It is where Jimmy was born, in Msimang Street, in 1945. Although he now lives in Diepkloof Extension — known in Soweto as Diepkloof Expensive — many of his relatives and friends have remained in Orlando East, where we visit the house Jimmy's father shares with his 72-year-old sister, Meisie Nkomo. The old man is not home but Meisie's son greets us. He presses white hands with discomforting, lingering enthusiasm, his eyes darting from head to toe in a rude body-search before he disappears into his room at the back of the house.

Meisie is watching a mid-morning soap opera called *Santa Barbara*. She turns the sound down, keeping an eye on screen events while describing her career as a cashier at the OK Bazaars in Johannesburg. 'One job for thirty years but they looked after me so beautifully when I retired, all the way, all the way.'

'My father was a man-about-town, very well known in Soweto in the fifties,' says Jimmy. 'Kelly Michaels: everybody knew him. He was in the bright spots and he didn't look after me; he looked after himself. Some people say you should look after your father when he is old and crippled, even if he never looked after you when you were young and helpless. I don't know why you must do that. Why should you?

'But never mind. Everybody did something good in his life. Kelly got passports for everybody in Soweto who wanted one. He could get a passport within three hours because he made friends with some old Afrikaner women in the passport office in Pretoria. He took flowers to them and told them sweet things, so they liked him and gave the passports quickly.'

We hear loud music at the back of the house, where Meisie's son is sitting in front of an ancient hi-fi. 'All of us played records on Saturday mornings. Everyone in Soweto, and still now they do it,' says Jimmy. 'Clean the garden and listen to jazz. People like Scratch Daddy, Sticks Hooper and the Jazz Crusaders.' The disc on the turntable is a recording of a jazz concert held in Tennessee during the 1940s. Jimmy's young cousin begins to duplicate the compère's twangy, deep-throated American words, and Jimmy joins in, accurately rendering every pause and syllable. Both laugh uproariously when the audience laughs, both lift imaginary saxophones to their lips when the music begins. As we stroll back to the house, Jimmy's voice retains traces of the American accent; it comes and goes throughout the day.

On the shelf of a display cabinet in Meisie's living room is a framed photograph of a beauty queen, her sash proclaiming Miss Mainstay 1989. 'That's my youngest,' says Meisie proudly. 'She's deceased now. She was shot in Soweto in 1990 on her way to work in Hillbrow, in her own car. It was the time of Mr Mandela's release: everybody going wild and somebody wanting that car.'

Another photograph, of Jimmy's grandfather in a suit and Homburg hat, was taken in President Street in downtown Johannesburg in the late 1930s. 'If you go into all these houses in Orlando you will find a picture just like this, taken at exactly the same place in President Street. One enterprising photographer stood there every day, all his life, taking these pictures. Everybody wanted one because nobody in Soweto had a camera.'

Meisie clutches her purse throughout our visit and Jimmy teases her: 'Leave it alone, mama; it's only money.' But later, driving away from the house, he says: 'That son of hers has never worked. He's twenty-five but like an old man already, sitting around with nothing to do. He does nothing, not even clean the garden. He takes everything from her. That's why she holds on to her purse so tight, as if it will walk away. It will if she doesn't hold it because her own son will take it.'

We drive down the road to drop in on Jomo Sono, a friend of Jimmy's. He owns Jomo Cosmos, one of Soweto's leading soccer teams. A well-heeled, revered figure in soccer-mad Soweto, he is lounging on leather as he studies a video of his team's latest match. His father, Eric Sono, captained Orlando

Pirates, a legendary team that continues to command respect throughout the country.

Jomo's house, extended many times, sprawls over the entire plot. 'It was my grandfather's four-roomed house originally, and then my father's,' he says. Jimmy asks if he is thinking of moving out of Soweto into the formerly whites-only suburbs of Johannesburg, as many of the township's prosperous residents are doing. It is a controversial debate and Jomo replies cautiously. 'I might go, because Soweto is too dangerous these days, but I will leave some relatives in this house, not sell it.'

A small dog barks at our heels. 'What's the matter with you?' Jimmy chastises it as we leave. 'Are you a racialistic dog, that you must bark at whites?' Driving on through the dirt roads of Orlando East, he jokes about the ire provoked by the migration of wealthy blacks from Soweto to white suburbs. 'Are we betraying somebody by moving, our ancestors, or our roots? I'm going to move, believe me or not,' he says. 'I want to go up with the Joneses, not the Sitholes or the Naidoos.'

Next stop is an old hall in Rathebe Street, now the Young Men's Christian Association, a community centre which holds dear memories for Jimmy. The foundation stone in the foyer was 'laid by James Donaldson DSO, benefactor of Africans...' It used to be the only place in Orlando offering a hot bath, explains Jimmy. 'Now many of the houses have bathrooms but nobody had one when I was growing up. There was one swimming pool in Soweto, Olympic size. Thousands were there every Saturday, queuing up to get in. So we couldn't stay long. We had to do it quickly, in and out. A lot of guys became good swimmers, or anyway good floaters.'

Inside the hall's tiny, empty theatre, Jimmy leaps on to the stage, bows deeply and blows kisses into the air. 'Maybe I'm too big and I've seen bigger halls but, boy oh boy, it was great in here back then. I was on this stage for school concerts. I was in those seats upstairs, watching Captain Marvel, Zola the Kid, the Manhattan Brothers, Miriam Makeba, Dolly Rathebe. Did I tell you I was with Dolly Rathebe yesterday? She was the first black woman from Soweto to become a star. And what a star! Shining for all of us. A wonderful, beautiful woman.'

The manager of the community centre for the past twenty-five years, Mandla Dube, says it has been the site of many dramatic events. 'The day before the students rose in 1976, the leaders of that march met here to discuss their strategy. I knew something big was on their minds but I never ask what they are doing, only when there is trouble. Three weeks ago, taxi men who were fighting in the street spilled into our hall. Three people were shot.

'We provide a safe haven for kids; they do not have many places to go in Soweto. Free movies on Mondays, but we have to turn most of them away. They come from all over. Children come to play music and dance. Some get famous. I know most of the bands that are playing in Soweto and Johannesburg because I saw them here when they were starting up.'

Posters on the noticeboard herald forthcoming attractions: Mr and Miss Funky, Mr and Miss Star Quality, Javas and Gospel Singers, Stereo Mc's Dr Vivaldi and Chaklas Le Roux, Mapunsula Girls, Boyz 11 Men, Hot Preppie and DJ Boyz, Ama Gents. Outside is a poster proclaiming a beauty contest at Diepkloof Hall: Miss Beauty and Proud and Mr Unique, to which the promoter has added the handwritten endorsement, 'Best prizes in town. Ask Miss Beauty and Brains.'

Several beauty pageants are staged every weekend in Soweto, and invariably attract large crowds. Known as BE (Black Elegance) and offering supporting roles for local musicians and choirs, the contests reflect urbanised Africa's enduring joys: music and dance. They also provide an income for promoters whose skills range from slick to shabby. A show that is billed to begin at 2.00 p.m. seldom gets going before 4.00 p.m. The children pay between R3 and R7 admission and wait patiently. 'Time doesn't count in Soweto,' says Jimmy. 'The kids have nothing else to do. They are all dressed to the core and happy to show themselves off while they wait for the promoters to arrive. Of course the promoters are just exploiting the kids. They don't pay the bands or the dancers. But it's OK because the children have something to do.'

We drive through the gates of Orlando's Old Age Day Care Centre, which is run by Jimmy's mother, Irene Ntintili. She started the home fifteen years ago after she found an old man living in a hole dug up near a toilet in Orlando East. It is lunchtime and the kitchen smells of spinach and onions, cooked by a team of smiling volunteers. Irene is out but accolades all over the wall of her office commemorate her remarkable career in the service of others: Woman of the Year 1989, Union of Jewish Women Award, Personality of the Year, a photograph of Irene with two of Mother Teresa's nuns. Jimmy jokes with the old people. 'No dying before the Christmas party,' he tells them. 'Make arrangements with the Lord,' retorts a bent figure.

We discuss Jimmy's altruistic pedigree. 'Only on the maternal side,' he says. 'My grandmother was the one who gave it all. She started a crèche for small children in Orlando.'

We talk about love across the colour barrier. Jimmy says black and white couples are viewed as much as a freak show in Soweto as in white suburbs. 'You must marry a black girl, not a white one, if you want to keep out of trouble.' He laughs, opens the top button of his shirt and draws the garment aside to reveal his chest. 'See these scars around my heart? They are stab wounds from a fine relationship with a black woman.

'Everybody thinks it is so strange to have a relationship with a white woman. They stare at you here in Soweto; they stare at you in Johannesburg. Big eyes, always watching. But they don't stare in Hamburg. When I met the parents of a white girlfriend in Germany, all they said was, "We thought you would be taller and slimmer." And I wish I was,' he says, patting his belly.

'The difference is the colour of the skin, that's all.' His voice rises indignantly. 'There are not a million people thinking like me but they're afraid to. "You're a white man in a black skin"; people tell me that. Many of my friends for years and years have been South African Jewish people. I met them there and here. They've been persecuted and now they're the most open and free. I was always bringing them on tours of Soweto. That's how I started Jimmy's Face to Face: I was doing it anyway with my friends. Foreigners love to see Soweto: it's the first tour they ask for. But white South Africans, no, they are afraid to come. People are afraid of each other, of their own reflections, even.'

We go to a shebeen, Theresa's Place. It looks like a regular house from the street and deliberately so, because selling liquor from private dwellings is a crime. A large room, built on at the back when Theresa started her business fifteen years ago, contains the kitchen and tables for patrons.

There are at least half a dozen shebeens in every Soweto street; an estimated 14 000 in Soweto. They have been the mainstay of social life in the township since the 1930s, when it was illegal to supply liquor to blacks. In the early 1960s, the government changed the law, allowing its own authorities to sell 'European' liquor to Africans through approved bottle stores and beer-halls. These drab establishments failed to defeat the intimate charm of shebeens, however, and most were destroyed during the students' uprising in 1976.

The majority of Soweto's shebeens are owned by middle-aged, divorced or widowed women, known as shebeen queens. In the past, they were invariably widows, given a free hand to reap the rewards of the lucrative liquor trade without competitors because township residents acknowledged that death had deprived them of breadwinners. The successful shebeen queen's most important credential is discretion, both in keeping quiet about what she hears and in selecting her patrons. She listens but never gossips, knows a lot about her patrons but never asks them questions. If she knows you well enough, she might grant you a short-term loan. Or you can leave part of your pay packet with her so that your wife doesn't spend it all. She is a shoulder to cry on; a calm voice in the turmoil of alcohol abuse.

Theresa's Place, an upmarket shebeen, sells beer, spirits, wine and champagne. At the other end of the social scale are shebeens selling concoction or mbamba, which is home-brewed beer containing brown bread, yeast and hops, amongst less orthodox ingredients. They also drink tots of mixed spirits, especially Fastmove (cane), and go beshugan (mad). A doctor at Baragwanath Hospital's casualty unit admits patients suffering from toxic psychosis every weekend. 'Whatever they put in that stuff, it kicks. They come in foaming at the month, confused, picking fights, shrieking or unconscious. One followed me around like a dog, licking my face, touching my hand, opening my fist. We put them on a well-balanced diet for ten days and they are better. They don't remember those ten days. When they come to they say, "I just remember going out with my friends. I knew I was at Bara when I saw the red blankets." '

Theresa's Place is busy at lunchtime because, unlike most shebeens, she serves food. We sit in her small lounge for a drink. 'Look at the curtains,' says Jimmy. 'Black women have great pride in their curtains.' They hang before us on a single window, intricate, voluminous and expensive; a ruched frill at the top, satin ribbon stitched on to floral fabric, gathered in a bow at the sill, with a white embroidered lace expanse beneath. Theresa joins us, giving change to a patron from a small plastic bank bag stored inside her bra.

She says the shebeen business isn't as good as it used to be. 'Lots of political prisoners started shebeens when they came home from prison in 1990. There are very many shebeens now. And there is too much violence. Some people buy their liquor in town and bring friends to their own houses, to drink at home. Some guys with guns got into my place, the ones who are stealing the cars. There was one patron with a Jetta. They went straight to him and demanded the keys. They took the car. They came back the same night, looking for girls, and started shooting. One patron was shot in the arm. This is what happens, all over, at weekends.

'Fortunately, my patrons respect me. I don't have trouble from inside, only outside, from criminals. Maybe it's the way I behave towards them. I don't sit down and drink with them, or my daughters who help me, because then they get attracted and want to take you by force. If girls come alone, some kind of girls, I say we are full because they are looking for men and will make trouble. My regulars know, if the police come, we are having a birthday party; there is no sale of liquor. But the police trap you. They send a man who says he is the friend of a patron and he buys with marked money. Then you can't deny it. You can tell the magistrate you were having a party but he fines you because of the plant.'

Driving to another shebeen, we pass the most popular drinking establishment in Soweto, Zak's Place in Diepkloof. A South African Breweries truck is off-loading crates of beer. 'The police raid regularly,' says Jimmy, 'but it doesn't matter because Zak-Zak sells well over a million rands of beer every month. He can afford the fines.'

Wandie's Place in Mofolo has a sign outside the entrance, 'No takkies, caps or weapons', which rules out the youth of Soweto. A television is perched on a shelf above the tables. South African leader F.W. de Klerk is being interviewed on CNN. 'I'm always surprised and truly pleased at the warm reception I sometimes get from black South Africans,' he tells the interviewer. The screen goes blank. A waiter dressed in black and white hurries to the set and hits it. The face returns. 'All hopes in the continent are on South Africa,' says De Klerk. 'We are the gateway to Africa.' Handel plays from a hi-fi. The place is formica-topped and business-like: a place to eat and drink in, like any other in South Africa, albeit at lower prices, amid plastic flowers and discordant colours.

Not everyone approves of Soweto's modern, sanitised shebeens. Hard-drinking, rough-talking old-timers lament the passing of the intimate shebeens of yesteryear, which they called 'home from home'. Journalist Doc Bikitsha uses the lingo of the 1950s to explain: 'Let me tell you, these chrome and glass and deep leather whatchamacallums don't hold a flickering candle to our establishments. They're so ... so industrial. They got no soul.'

Another black journalist, Joe Louw, says: 'With the demise of the shebeen, and the rise of the colour TV tavern and the disco-fied inn, came a sad deletion from our culture — the death of conversation, of the jokes and the tell-tales, the gossip and the creativity that nurtured language and immortalised the thousand-and-one characters and their improvisations which brought cheer to life even in the worst times.'

Jimmy tells us about James Sofazonke Mpanza, born nearby at 957 Orlando East in a house which is sometimes a stop on his tour. 'There were thousands of people without homes. In the 1940s, their anger rose up. Thousands of men, women and children, led by Mpanza, left the location and camped on vacant municipal ground nearby. It was called Shanty Town, the first of many squatter movements.'

Mpanza was born in 1889: 'Only three weeks younger than Hitler,' he would point out whenever interviewed. Although he collected rent from the squatters and would not allow anybody to trade among them but himself, Mpanza achieved heroic stature in Soweto. 'He was a great politician,' says Jimmy. 'He used to say, "Let any man who is against people drinking in shebeens stand up and say it publicly — and he will surely be stoned to death." '

Reginald Bolowu is another famous name in Orlando East. 'He was the genius of South Africa but nobody knew about him outside the location,' says Jimmy. 'In Standard One they couldn't handle him so they sent him to Standard Three. Then the teachers sent him on because again he was too clever. In Standard Nine he passed matric. He went to university but complained that the teachers didn't know what they were doing. He wanted to do nuclear physics but they couldn't teach him that so he came home and worked for the revolution. Then he went to Sweden and became the number one nuclear physicist there. He came back to South Africa once for a conference, representing physics for Sweden, not for South Africa. He is a Swedish scientist but he was born in Soweto. Ask anyone in Orlando East: they remember Reginald Bolowu.'

We eat tasty mutton stew rather than chicken wings, served with pap and salads. 'It's OK to spill a bit of your food down your shirt or on the floor,' says Jimmy. 'We are expected to do it at every meal, to give something to our ancestors. If you give an old African a glass of whisky, very precious, he will spill some on the floor for his ancestors.'

As we eat, Jimmy philosophises. 'Sowetans have become too bourgeois. If we can live on chicken wings and pap, why don't we use our money to get ahead, be smart, have our children in good schools, instead of spending everything we earn on shoes and clothes to show off?'

Supporting this point, Jimmy later stops his bus on the side of a road near the symbolic tomb of Hector Petersen, the first child killed by police during the students' uprising in 1976. Hailing a smartly dressed boy of Hector's age, Jimmy asks him: 'How much did your shoes cost?' The 13-year-old looks down at his green suede footwear and replies: 'Five hundred rands at the Carlton Centre.'

Soweto's busiest market place is at the central taxi terminal, opposite Baragwanath Hospital. We wander among traders selling fruit and vegetables, clothing old and new, watches, trinkets and sweets from makeshift stalls. Behind is a brick shopping centre, its pavement crowded with vendors.

Jimmy stops a shopper whose face is smeared with a pale granular substance. 'What is that muti (medicine) for?' he asks. 'Sun cream,' she replies. We examine the wares of Dr D.C. Shezi, a sangoma wearing a benign expression under a green knitted cap, who says he makes R200 on a busy day. His mutis are packaged in soft drink bottles, with labels bearing his photograph and trade name, Soweto Black Medicine. Jimmy stands beside Dr Shezi and launches into a sales pitch, to the amusement of passers-by. 'This is the cure-all,' he says of a liquid resembling muddy water. 'You will never know what it contains because the sangoma is not allowed to tell you.' Dr Shezi nods sagely. 'You take it for a few weeks, for potency problems, menstruation pain, backache or diarrhoea, and it works. Yes, indeed, it works. You are so healthy, it hurts. You are so potent, it's not fun.'

Three Zulu women — in traditional quilted skirts with deep scarification scars on their faces — stroll by, stopping to finger T-shirts bearing the names of American and Sowetan football teams, LA Rangers and Orlando Pirates. A shop selling sugar and cigarettes displays tombstones in the window. Next door is the most expensive clothing store in Soweto. 'Don't try to bargain on the prices,' warns Jimmy.

We follow him into a shebeen housed in a tent, which serves hot food and ice cold beer despite the absence of electricity. Inside is a blazing brazier to cook the food, and several refuse bins filled with ice to cool the drinks. 'If you're wondering why the rubbish lies around the streets, here's the answer,' says Jimmy. 'The dustbins are in the shebeens.'

Young men in caps and takkies are playing a game of dice outside. 'They're gambling,' says Jimmy, who used to sell food at the taxi rank and knows everyone's business there. 'Watch this.' He takes a R5 note and strides into their midst. Grabbing the dice, he flings the ivory squares on to the dirt in a flourish of loud Xhosa words and vigorous dance steps. The youths stand back. Jimmy wins with a yelp of triumph, scoops up the money and runs towards his bus, pursued by shouting teenagers who want a chance to win their money back. He tells them he's going to use it to buy biscuits for poor children. They look unimpressed. One of them sidles up to a pretty American tourist and tells her quietly, 'I want to marry you.' Ever watchful, Jimmy sprints to her side and shouts, 'Time to go.'

Further down Soweto's main road is another produce market, with two wire pens filled with sheep and goats. The animals are sold in large numbers every Friday and Saturday for funeral and wedding feasts or for sacrificial ceremonies organised by sangomas.

Jimmy points out houses that have tents or awnings staked beside them, each with a tall, narrow hired lavatory. 'That's where the weddings and funerals are this weekend,' he says. 'You can tell which houses are having funerals by the plastic baby baths that are there on the ground outside the gate for the mourners to wash their hands when they come from the grave. They have to wash away the bad spirits.'

We stop at one house where the members of a funeral club, dressed in black with blue pinafores, are in attendance. An old woman sits on a chair, sobbing. Her 19-year-old grandson was fatally stabbed a week earlier during a fight in a house a few doors away.

The mourners are at the graveside. The women from the funeral club have prepared the feast, laid out on a long table: biscuits, fruit juice, salads to go with the pap and meat being cooked on a brazier. 'We're here for togetherness,' says one of the attendants. 'When there is a death, we give money collected from all our members every month. A cow or two goats will be slaughtered, or we buy meat from a butchery if the deceased died a violent death. You don't slaughter when the death results from unnatural causes.'

Cars begin to park beside the house and we leave. Half an hour later when we drive past, a queue of mourners, clutching paper plates, stretches down the street. Another funeral cortège rolls by: a dazzling pink hearse with silvery highlights gleaming from its paintwork, a matching fifties Chevrolet following behind, and a long line of cars, all with their headlights on.

At Mandela Village in Diepkloof — a squatter camp teeming with humanity from Nelson Mandela's birthplace, the Transkei — Jimmy prepares to hand out the biscuits he has bought with his gambling gains. It is a ritual the local children know well, and they run to greet him. 'Stand in lines,' he tells them. 'Little

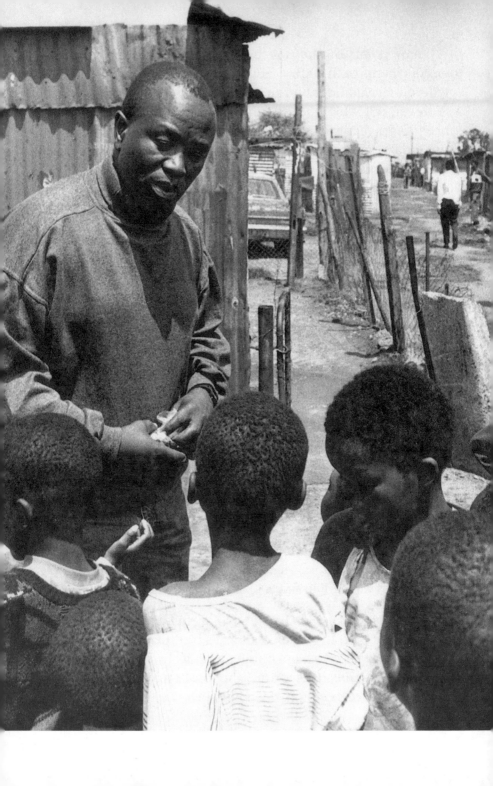

Tour operator Jimmy Ntintili with children from Mandela Village, a squatter settlement in Diepkloof.
Photograph: Louise Gubb

ones on this side, big ones there.' They are having fun, jumping and laughing, as is Jimmy.

Inside one of the shelters, a tiny partitioned room made from wood and corrugated iron, is a young woman and her six children. 'No husband,' says Jimmy irritably after questioning her. 'Typical. Every girl in Soweto has at least one baby before she's twenty, but no husband.' He explains that she earns money by selling vegetables. 'No more babies,' he tells her. The home is neat and clean, its walls papered with bright advertisements cut from magazines. A candle is wedged into a wine bottle for light; a small paraffin stove cooks the food. Houses such as this one often catch fire, says Jimmy, not least because small boys cannot resist the lure of matches. A large Burns Unit was recently opened at Baragwanath to tend the many victims, mainly children, of fires in overcrowded places.

We drive to Dube Hostel, a complex of bleak men-only dormitories built to accommodate migrant workers. Thirty-two men share each of the barracks. Their beds are barely a yard apart, with ragged curtains hanging between in a forlorn attempt at privacy. There is a brief altercation at the doorway of one of the blocks, between Jimmy and a member of the Inkatha Freedom Party (IFP), the political base of South Africa's Zulu people. Virtually all the hostels in Soweto are Zulu strongholds, containing men who are workers by day but often warriors by night in the deadly battle for political supremacy that rages nationwide between those loyal to the ANC and their IFP rivals.

Hair 'saloons', as they are known throughout Soweto, are advertised outside many houses. As plentiful as shebeens, they specialise in hair 'relaxants'. It is a euphemism for straightening techniques, a sensitive issue among Black Consciousness adherents who decry attempts to straighten black hair on the grounds that the culprits are trying to look like whites. In the front seat of the bus alongside Jimmy sits a young black man whose stretched hair is arranged in elaborate dreadlocks. Though born in Soweto, he has spent the past nine years in exile in America. He now lives in Johannesburg; it is his first visit to the township, though his parents still live there, since returning to South Africa five months earlier. A group of youths at the roadside — takkies, caps and two rings in the right ear lobe — wave as they see the black occupants at the front of our bus, then rub thumbs and forefingers together to symbolise money on spotting whites in the back. Jimmy yells from the window: 'How're you guys doing?' 'Swell,' they reply in unison.

'If you want a good story about Soweto,' says Jimmy, 'ask the mothers what they think their children are doing all day, and then see what the kids are actually doing. A Hyde and Jekyll story.'

Another shebeen, this time Mathilda's Place in White City Jabavu. It consists of three rooms, a kitchen dominated by a large fridge, Mathilda's bedroom, and a lounge with splendid curtains frothing from a single window. 'Not anybody comes here,' says Jimmy as we crowd into the tiny sitting-room. 'Mathilda's is for intellectuals.' The shebeen queen stands at the door listening. She is a middle-aged woman whose face bears the remnants of beauty, as well as burn scars from an ugly incident years ago, when she was set alight by a woman who believed Mathilda was having an affair with her husband.

'Twenty people will sit in here every night, believe me or not,' says Jimmy. 'Doctors, lawyers, businessmen. Smart cars will be parked outside. Some of these men will slip their car keys under the sofa cushion in case thieves come in and demand the BMW or the Jetta. Then they will say, "Oh, it belongs to a patron who is coming back just now." But another will put his BMW keys on the table so everyone can see he has a big car. Guys are guys, no matter what race.

'If I come here with takkies that stink and a scar on my face, Mathilda will be quick at the door, saying the place is full. But really Mathilda's has no closing time and is never too full for her regulars.'

Back in the street, a man is urinating against a wall, his body pressed close to it in hope of discretion. Opposite is a slogan, neatly printed on another wall: 'Please behave yourself. This is not a toilet.'

We pass a large group of women, uniformly dressed and walking briskly. They are cashiers returning from the Saturday shift at a supermarket in Johannesburg. All carry grocery bags — which Jimmy calls plastics — bearing the chain store's emblem. 'Where are you going in such a rush?' Jimmy yells from his window. 'To a birthday party,' replies one in full stride. 'We're late.'

At Club 707 in Orlando West, a disco, we watch a rehearsal for the evening's beauty contest. At first it is a serious business, with haughty contestants mincing up and down the ramp. Then music strikes. The dark, cave-like room springs to life. Bodies leap from chairs in shadowy corners and start jiving, up to the ramp and on to it. Young employees carrying beer crates leave their duties to join in. The models, swept aside, dance towards the curtains backstage. Everyone is rocking and rolling.

When the music stops, they return to their seats and chores. The models return to the catwalk. An atmosphere of acute expectation prevails. Everyone is waiting for Saturday night to reveal its epic moments.

Outside, people are hurrying along the streets as darkness falls. We drive past Spoons' Place. 'This is the shebeen for clevers, the criminals who steal the cars,' says Jimmy. 'Spoons talks like his patrons, recited English: they're saying so much but they've said nothing yet.' The shebeen king is standing in front of his house, gazing down the road in search of his patrons, waiting for Saturday night to begin. Jimmy hails him. 'A very good evening to you, sir,' Spoons replies grandly. 'Welcome all, for fun and laughter. Be cool and collected. Drive carefully, my buddies.'

7

Mama Mabala

▼▼▼

Michael is a cheerful looking 15-year-old whose smile conceals a wounded heart. A boy his own age plunged a knife through his chest, puncturing the vital organ. He survived only as a result of emergency surgery at Baragwanath Hospital, where doctors are confronted with so many stabbed hearts that they routinely rip open patients' chests in the corridor on the way to theatre so as to release trapped blood that in most cases causes death.

The savage fight between Michael and a boy he still calls his friend occurred a long time ago but Michael never returned to the hospital to have his multiple stitches removed. They are still in his chest, like a tattooed railway line, though the sutures which mended the gash in his heart dissolved automatically. The reason he never returned to the hospital is fear: Michael is a street child who distrusts a helping hand. He has been beaten and betrayed too many times to risk an honest exchange of human care.

Street children like Michael number an estimated 25 000 in South African cities. They are overlooked by the state's welfare agencies. None of the established children's homes will accept them. Rescue and rehabilitation missions are left to volunteer and church initiatives like a white-run organisation called Twilight Children, which operates in Johannesburg. 'When these kids first come to us, they're like animals,' says a spokesperson for Twilight Children of the physically and emotionally battered black waifs who roam Johannesburg's streets and alleys in survival packs, scrounging for food and fighting each other for scraps of clothing and other dustbin discoveries.

Though admirably robust in its intentions, Twilight Children achieves limited success in persuading the city's ragamuffins to test the alien dimensions of human warmth. The organisation offers educational games, showers, the chance to exchange filthy clothes for clean garments and to eat nourishing food, but few street kids accept the kindness. Most of those who enter Twilight Children's doors behave abominably, throwing food at each other and ignoring the entreaties of volunteer workers. 'You should see how they behave when they first arrive here,' says a Twilight woman, explaining that the kids sniggering contemptuously and smearing chocolate mousse over each other as we speak are tame examples of street children. 'They lie on the floor, kick and spit and stuff food in their mouths by the fistful. The little ones huddle in the corner, cry when you go near them, snatch their food and then run back to the streets. Even if we're only achieving minimal success, it's something we have to keep working at because once these boys grow into adults they can't beg as effectively as children do or earn money from helping shoppers find parking. If they're totally unsocialised it's almost impossible for them to find legitimate jobs so they're inevitably absorbed in the criminal element.'

Food for the Twilight centres is donated, after the sell-by date, from perishables in a store catering to the affluent end of the country's white market. 'The children have a pretty exotic diet here,' says a volunteer. 'Tonight it's pap, cabbage with cream on top, raspberry tart and strawberry milk. Often they'll have smoked salmon or pâté or prawns in cottage cheese.' Some of the kids, knowing which store supplies their outlandish rations, periodically help themselves directly from the deli's shelves. Openly flaunting their shop-lifting activities, they ignore warnings from a management aghast at their ungrateful behaviour.

It is in the realm of social values that Twilight Children meets its greatest challenge. The difference between right and wrong is unfamiliar to these kids; an abandoned distinction in the battle for a tolerable existence. Life has used them so roughly that they keep people at arm's length with insolent comments and stares. 'Some of the kids have been living in the streets for years. They were born in the streets and hovels of Soweto and other townships of parents who are prostitutes or drunks. They have learnt to grab what they can, regardless of the consequences for others. Some of them have left home because of terrible poverty or physical abuse from fathers or stepfathers.'

'Virtually all their human contact on the streets is negative,' says another Twilight volunteer. 'People kick them when they beg, or beat them up. Some pour water on them from flat windows in winter. At best, they're pointedly ignored by the public. This reinforces their insecurity and alienation. We try to break the glue-sniffing addiction which most of them, even seven-years-olds, have adopted as an escape from the harsh realities of hunger and cold and loneliness. The glue can ultimately kill them. At the very least we can make these poor kids aware that a few people do care about them.'

The wizened faces of dustbin kids are a feature of many cities worldwide. Charles Dickens's *Oliver Twist* and Victor Hugo's *Les Miserables* immortalised their pitiful plight in literature. A sharply increasing phenomenon in South Africa, research indicates that around one-third are classified as 'abandoning' rather than 'abandoned'. They are said to have made a wilful departure from homes that have not always been severely abusive environments. Saying they prefer the streets, these boys appear to have actively set out with the intention of shaping a different life for themselves.

'There is no doubt that such environmental factors as poverty, rural-to-urban migration, civil strife and family violence play a central role in the genesis of street children,' says sociologist Dr J. Kirk Felsman. 'Many children in the developing countries, however, share such fate and circumstances and the vast majority are not in the streets. In the abandoning child, these factors do not fully account for their being in the streets.'

Dr Felsman advises that rehabilitation programmes for street children must take into account 'the enormous amount of strength and resiliency these children often possess. For example, the term vagrant implies a sense of aimless wandering. The daily lives of many street children, however, reflect patterns of organisation and are quite purposeful and goal-directed. Children who engage in shining shoes, selling papers or guarding cars are employed, albeit informally or even illegally. Furthermore, successful begging is hard work. It is competitive and it requires intelligence, creativity and physical stamina. Many of the survival strategies of street children daily demonstrate healthy, competent, adaptive behaviour. Thus to characterise them as helpless and powerless emphasises only their vulnerabilities. To be of genuine help to these children, social policy must respect and foster their strength, providing greater opportunity for the expression of their demonstrated competence.'

Much research on street children is being conducted by people who seek to alter their tragic destiny in countries all over the world. One teenage glue-sniffer told an interviewer: 'You can create a thousand institutions but you'll never hold him because he loves freedom and adventure more than blankets and good manners. But all the world can be transformed and a new man born in him when you say, "Brother, give me your hand." '

* * *

Enter Mama Mabala. She is illiterate; answers to the complex problems of helping street children come to her intuitively. She knows you have to hug children if you hope to rescue them from a world in which innocence has been outlawed.

Ethel Mabala has well-utilised mothering skills, having raised ten happy children of her own. She looks after a dozen grandchildren during the week while their parents are at work. But that is not what sets her apart. Over the past year, she has opened her heart and the doors of her humble home to the street children of Johannesburg. At least seventy ragged urchins − the number varies from day to day − now live in her four-roomed house in Mofolo North, Soweto.

She hadn't planned to share her home with them: such an idea would have been unthinkable in abstract. 'It just happened,' she says. 'I was seeing these young boys in the streets, all over, begging and being drunk from glue. I am driving with the taxi and watching them for a long time, whenever I go to town. My heart is hurting. I ask some people, where do they sleep? Nobody knows.

'So one time I was passing with a taxi. It was not the first time I saw a young boy running with the glue, and a car hit him. I was crying, too much. When the taxi stopped for me to go to him, I see the child running away, holding his leg. The

Mama Mabala: Soweto's extraordinarily kind surrogate mother to numerous street urchins.
Photograph: Victor Matom

car is gone. I shout to the boy. He does not hear me. Another one, at the corner of Rissik and Wolmarans Streets, I see dirty, thin like my finger, lying on the road, nearly dead. I hold him and give him water. Then I see his heart is not moving.

'I prayed to God: what must I do? After that, carrying the Bible, I go to where many of them stay, Rissik and Wolmarans, standing on the place where the boy died. There were five children near me, parking the cars. I call to them and they run. I said, "Don't run away. Come. I love you." They came. I read from the Bible and ask them, "Do you love God?" They said yes. I said, "Can I feed you?" They used to get food from the dustbins of the restaurants. First time they didn't say they were hungry. I go again, many times. They asked me to bring pap and meat because they do not like the white food.

'I went twice a week. Many other boys come every time. There is no more money for the taxi and the meat. I went with pap. Then they say they want to come with me. I say, no, they cannot come to stay at my house. It is small. No money. But they ask me again, many times.

'I go home, ask my husband, Mike. He is a good man. He says, "Bring them on Sunday, the day of our daughter's wedding. We go to church." I take the taxi to bring them to Mofolo, too many of them. The taxi doesn't want to take them all, but I beg. We went to church, cooked nice food, talked to my husband about God. After, we take money to give them for the taxi. They go.

'In the night — it is raining — we hear singing at 2.00 a.m. They are outside, knocking and singing and crying. "We are cold. Somebody took our blankets, Mama." I said to my husband, "Where can we put these children?" He prayed to God. I let them all in, more than before, so many children I did not count. I ask where did they get money for the taxi and they said, "No, we walked." The clothes are wet. We take them off and hang in the kitchen, light the fire, give some little bit of tea. There are no blankets for all. We take curtains from the window. They lie on the floor, so happy.'

'The next night they were back, and the night after that,' says Mike, a labourer. 'We told them we had no space for them but they wouldn't go away. We have nothing here and we are struggling. But they just love my wife.'

The Mabalas have miraculously found living space for seventy-three children — at the last count. The kids come and go as they please, often returning with friends from the streets. Mothers in strife-torn townships like Thokoza and Katlehong, frightened for their children's safety, send them to stay with the Mabalas. The youngest boy, Lucky, aged five, was left on their doorstep by a destitute woman.

At night, Ethel and Mike sleep in a tiny room partitioned off the lounge. In the early days, they lay awake for hours, unused to the sound of so many chattering voices. Half-a-dozen girls, rescued from prostitution, share the rest of the room. Two dozen of the youngest boys sleep on the kitchen floor. 'You must not get up in the night; there is no place to walk,' says Mama. The rest lie in the garage, tightly packed together in blankets which they've been taught to fold neatly and stack in a corner during the day, when the ramshackle place becomes a classroom.

Mornings are chaotic, with up to eighty bodies sharing one tiny bathroom. Before he leaves for work, Mike fills several basins and buckets with water, in which those of the children who are not in a hurry for the toilet wash and brush their teeth. The sound of all this ablution activity is deafening. So is the spiritual cleansing that follows. They line up to sing hymns in discordant voices, and shout prayers up to Heaven as if God might not hear them.

Much nudging and kicking and helpless laughter precedes their arrangement into classes. Two of the Mabala daughters and two local youths with better than average secondary schooling teach English and Maths to groups of fifteen at a time. Four women from Mama's church arrive every morning to prepare food in giant cooking pots and do the laundry. Ethel and Mike's bed is stacked high with clothes to be washed during the day. At night, piles of clean garments surround the couple's bed: there is nowhere else to put them.

'We are doing it for God and praying He will help us,' says Ethel. 'Before, when there was no money for food, the boys were going mad, throwing things, windows broken, and kicking the pots. Some went on the roof, jumping, very naughty. I call them to come and pray to God for food and some do. Now, they all come. Yesterday there was no food, only tea and some little bread in the morning. They are very hungry. They like to eat too much. We prayed. They were calm. I said God will provide and they know it is true. That's why they run to your car when you come this morning. They are so happy. They know you will give money for pap and sugar.

'They are good children now, still fighting, but not too much now. We allow them to go to town. They are free. Always they come back, with others. We try to find the parents. After going home, they come back: the parents say the child doesn't want to stay. They say they want to stay with their sister, Mama Mabala. One boy told his mother he will run away from her, disappear, if she does not allow him to return. That mother was too much drunk every days. Boyfriends at night. I say to the mother, don't worry, I will have him. And she is happy for that.

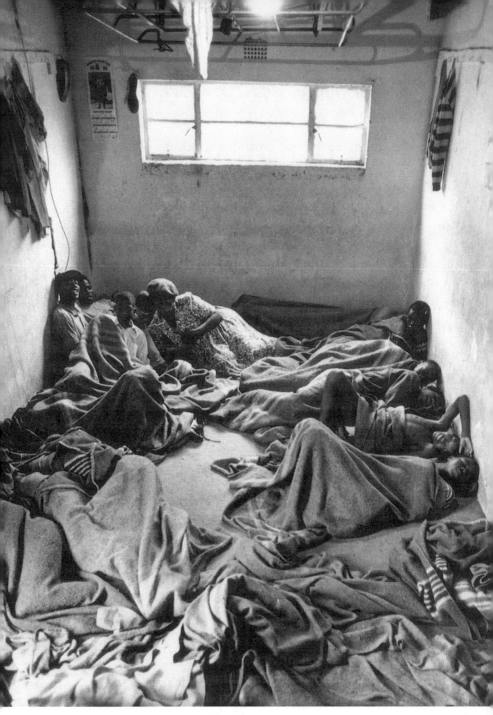

Mama Mabala whispers to some of the seventy street children who share her tiny home in Mofolo. The photograph was taken in the early morning, when the boys nearest the camera were still asleep under their blankets.

Photograph: Victor Matom

'Sometimes the white people from the church bring money. Somebody gave many chairs. They go one-in-one on top of the other, up in the yard, when there is no school. For school, the children sit on one and make one the desk, to write on.'

We are talking in the car with the windows closed, the only place at 555 Usuthu Street where we can hear each other above the clamour of children demanding attention. A small boy taps on the window beside Mama Mabala. She winds it down immediately. He wants a pencil. She gets out and takes his hand: the interview must wait, not the child. Another boy stands at the window, crying, soon after she settles back in the car. He has cut his foot climbing on a barbed wire fence. Mama gets out and presses his wet face to her belly, lifts him up and carries him to the bathroom.

Surprisingly, Mama's kids are eager to tell their stories when we interrupt a lesson and invite them to do so. Observing classroom etiquette, their hands shoot into the air, remaining stretched above tense backs and impatient expressions until the teacher calls their names. The room is silent as each boy stands up and speaks. Twelve-year-old Thuso had a stepmother who didn't like him. His own mother died when he was eight. The surrogate used his father's money to buy clothes for her own children and not for him. Fourteen-year-old Zazi's mother 'passed away and there was nobody to help me.' Eight-year-old Bheki says his mother and father went away. He helped a man in a scrapyard in exchange for food and a place to sleep but the man got cross with him one day and beat him, so he went to live in the streets. Thirteen-year-old Lawrence had a stepfather 'hitting and fighting with me. Then he hit my mother. She ran away. I got another stepfather, same again. My mother ran away again. I did not find her and I ran to the streets.'

Leonard, who is thirteen, lived in Kimberley. 'With another boy, I took money for the train to Johannesburg, just to see. Then no money to go home. My uncle told me not to go back. My mother is sick and drinking and doesn't want me there. I go to live in the street, parking cars. The glue makes me sick. I come here to my mother, Mama Mabala.' Ten-year-old Bongang speaks very little English so Mama translates his story. 'The thing making him go to the streets is a woman fighting with his mother. That lady hit his mother. So Bongang feel he must hurt that lady. So he went to her house and the husband chased him and said he was going to send other tsotsis to kill his mother. So Bongang think he better run away. If he is not at home, they will not kill his mother. So he go to the streets. Sometimes he go home to see his mother but she has run away. Nobody knows where she is.' The subject of this pathetic tale, now perched on Mama Mabala's lap with a look of smug self-importance on his dirty face, gabbles to her urgently. She adds: 'He wants to tell you he is going to school for the first time, here at my house.'

It is clear from all their stories that Soweto's street children leave home when the bond with their mother is broken, either through death, hopeless alcoholism or her disappearance. Sixteen-year-old Solomon says he was always stealing. His father beat him and locked him in a room. Then his mother died and he ran away. Does he still steal? He does not understand the question but nods, looking hurt and confused as they all laugh, except one child who rushes up to the interviewer. Cupping his hands around her face, he explains imploringly: 'He means no, he does not steal. Write it, write it.' Then he too laughs, hugging Mama Mabala on the way back to his seat.

Inside each sad ragamuffin dwells a laughing, loving son. 'They want to sit on me every time, one on this leg, one there, one on my back, even the big ones. They are heavy but I leave them. I want to tell them they are human beings with love in their hearts; love for God, love for me and Mike, love for these others, love for the wife and children later. Some, they help each other now. They help me. They help Mike. We forget some of the names but not the faces.

'Some of the children were having very bad lives at home. One — his mother adopted him when she found him in a toilet — ran away because her children didn't want him. They called a witch to give him a big fright from the grave of his mother, the one who gave birth to him but left him in the toilet. He was on the streets for eight years. Too much glue, very bad. When he was here, a long time, every morning he don't wake up. He sleeps like a stone. Now he's coming all right. No more glue.

'When they start to stay with us, they are fighting day and night. They had vulgar words. They did not say thank you. I tell them, when they are all watching TV, "Mike likes TV too much, every night he used to sit to watch it. Now he can't see it because too many children are there; Mike can't find a place to sit." I tell them this again and then some of the boys listen and get up and say to Mike, "Do you want to sit here?" Mike sits, because it is learning for them. But he says to me after, "It's OK, let them watch. I give up now." But I say it again to the children sometimes, because they must learn to do good for Mike.

'My husband, he is a very good man. He talks to the children. He tells them stealing, glue, violence, it's the work of the devil. And they are listening to him. Before, some boys were fighting with Coca-Cola bottles. They break it and stab other children, maybe once or twice a week. We never tell even one boy to leave because every one is good. We tell them, talk to them, all the time talking. Now it is only the new ones who try to kill others.

'We deny some things they say. When they say we are like this because of our parents, we say, no, it is not them. It is you. It is in yourself to be bad or good. You can be that way or that way. Then they pray to ask God to forgive them and help them.

'When they say we are like this because the political leaders or because the whites, we say you must pray for peace, not talk about political leaders, this one and this one. Although they have done you wrong, they didn't make you to sniff glue: not the parents, not the political leaders, not the whites. The parents want to grow you up and educate you. They did not manage. It was too hard. Now you do it by yourself. Come on, pray.

'These boys are clever, all of them. The ones who are not clever are staying at home, even if there is violence, family hate and quarrels. Somebody will give food at home, aunty or some others. They are not starving at home. They run away because they want to have fun, some better things. But in the streets there is glue. All the others take it so they all do it. Then they are losing themselves, thinking only of hate and stealing and fighting.

'We tell them to forgive everybody. Some are calling to see their sisters and fathers; some who did not want to see them before. Jesus said, "I have loved thee with an everlasting love." I want these children to love their parents. They can stay here but they must go to the others and forgive them. I tell them they will not find peace if there is hate in their hearts. There is no peace for them until they forgive everybody and make a new feeling in their hearts.'

8

African Magic

D r Bonna Sara Mashele is preparing a shrine for one of her
clients. She is a tall, heavy woman, who lowers herself
awkwardly to her knees in order to adjust the holy objects
gathered in a corner of her consulting room.

A framed picture of the Pope playing carpet bowls hangs
over the collection of religious artefacts: a painted plastic
statue of the Virgin Mary, two smaller representations of
Christian saints, a copper chalice, three brass candle holders,
one of them cast in the image of a snake. Hanging behind the
lit candles is a photograph of Sara Mashele waving a whisk of
animal tails as she sits in a motor boat surrounded by the heads
of four goggled divers whose mission, she explains, was to find
a body under the water. A large potted plant, decorated with
brightly coloured ribbon and raffia flowers, plus a cabbage
gone to seed, its tightly packed green centre surrounded by
frilly mauve leaves, complete the display of objects rendered
precious by their associations.

She puts her jewelled hands together, praying silently for a
while, then begins to mumble in a voice that does not seem to
be hers. The sound becomes a chant, growing louder until she

stops, dropping her arms wearily to her sides, numerous bangles of silver and ivory sliding down to her wrists with a clank. Heaving herself up from the floor, she stands briefly on the hide of an impala, under which are posters proclaiming the funerals of Chris Hani and Helen Joseph, two heroes of the African National Congress's struggle against white domination in South Africa.

Sara Mashele is a diviner and herbalist, a traditional healer known to blacks as a sangoma and to most whites as a witchdoctor. A devout Roman Catholic, she has lived in Soweto all her adult life. Her work over the last twenty years has been conducted in consulting rooms in downtown Johannesburg's Rissik Street, where she recently installed a fax machine in order to counsel clients from a distance when necessary. She says she is entitled to call herself doctor in English because, as an eminent sangoma, she has been accorded the distinction of the title bonna by her peers, which is the equivalent of doctor in her own language, Sotho. Many of Sara Mashele's patients are whites, particularly businessmen, who come to her derelict rooms in Africa House to consult her about their money, career, health and love problems, as well as to seek her guidance in choosing the horses to back in major races, like the lucrative Durban July Handicap.

Sara's psychic powers are widely proclaimed. Some clients in her waiting room do not wish to discuss the subject, understandably. Blacks believe the ancestral spirits get angry if a sangoma's marvels are revealed, but others are willing to describe her supernatural skills. One businessman, still in love with a former girlfriend, consulted Sara about the woman, who was engaged to marry a new lover in Canada. Sara consulted her divining bones and relayed an urgent message to the ditched suitor: he must telephone his sweetheart immediately. This he did, with some trepidation, to discover that she was miserable in Canada and longing to return to him.

Sara Mashele's work takes her all over the country, sometimes in search of rare plants required for her healing mutis, and sometimes to dispense spiritual or herbal cures to clients in other cities. 'I flew to Cape Town every week for many months last year for a Portuguese man whose brain was damaged in an accident,' she says. 'He is OK now.' Did she find the body under the water on the occasion when the photograph in her consulting room was taken? 'Of course,' she replies disdainfully. 'The frogmen couldn't find it; that's why they called me.'

Her divination and herbalist skills are widely sought, even at the exorbitant prices she charges. Whether there is a sliding scale based on the wealth of her clients is hard to establish, but one woman who was expecting to pay R65 for a bone-throwing session was astonished to be told she owed R120. Lifting her handbag, the client confessed she was unsure if she had that much money in her purse. Sara Mashele watched with a wry look as the wallet was opened. It contained two R50 notes and one R20: exactly the amount required. 'Coincidence, or what?' the client asked herself.

The patient for whom the shrine has been built in Sara's consulting room is a white medical doctor, a surgeon, who suffered a serious head injury in a car accident six months previously. He was asked by his wife during a lucid conversation if he wished to try alternative medicine. Rejecting acupuncture, he agreed to enlist the skills of a sangoma.

Before leaving her rooms to visit the surgeon, Sara unlocks a walk-in safe filled with shelves of muti. A tangle of dried grasses, leaves and tree bark lies on the floor but Sara pulls the door behind her; the contents of her medicine storeroom must remain secret, she says, or the healing spirits may become offended and withdraw her gifts. Some of the muti ingredients are bought from herbalists' shops in Soweto, and others are collected in the fields, forests and mountains of the Transvaal. Sara says the spirits sometimes lead her to desired herbs about which she previously had no knowledge.

Soweto's herb shops sell everything from rare iguana fat to snake skin, sunburnt beetles and spiders, lion lard, dried crocodile liver and baboon testicles. To give a person security, the herbalist administers a portion of the body of a tortoise; for swiftness, the sinew of a hare. Many of the remedies might be termed sympathetic magic: to ensure a good journey, for example, the prescription is made from a root that sends out many runners and therefore knows its way.

Dozens of brightly coloured powders, ground from untold herbs and flesh, offer cures for most ailments, including sexual impotence, headaches and unrequited love. When a wife suspects her husband is turning to a new woman, she buys a tasteless powder and adds it to his food in the belief that his affection will return. If a woman suffers from the condition which translates as 'unpregnancy', she inhales a snuff that promotes fertility. A fast seller is a powder made from lion paws and bought by the mothers of timid children to ward off bullying at school. Sangomas claim their healing knowledge was acquired from Southern Africa's original inhabitants, the Khoisan, who were the masters of this art.

Next to lion bits with courageous properties, crocodile parts are highly prized by herbalists. Considered a mighty and magical animal, the crocodile has teeth which renew themselves, he feeds on living flesh, and his hide deflects bullets. Two white hunters who killed a crocodile some years ago cut it up in a busy Johannesburg street and sold every bit of the beast to eager muti dealers. A reporter from *The Star*, a

Bonna Sara Mashele is a diviner and herbalist, a traditional healer known to blacks as a sangoma and to most whites as a witchdoctor.
Photograph: Derek Hudson

Johannesburg newspaper, wrote a front page story on the event, concluding: 'It would be easy to have a laugh at the muti man's expense, but wiser men than I have found that some of the muti men's wares are medically sound.'

Sara Mashele's patient, the surgeon, is sitting in a wheelchair at a Johannesburg clinic when she arrives to treat him. Rummaging in her handbag, she produces a variety of mutis and containers, a couple of animal bones and some porcupine quills.

A dark brown substance in a small bottle is smeared with a quill on to the patient's head and spastic left arm and leg. It emits a sweet aroma, mingled with the smell of damp soil. He asks if it contains cinnamon or lavender but Sara does not reply. She balances two tiny homemade candles, which look as if they are moulded from marzipan, on a miniature oval alabaster dish, and lights them. The flames flare briefly, leaving thick black smoke surging from the embers. Sara passes the dish to and fro beneath the surgeon's nose. Then she takes a quill, inserts it through the hole in one of the animal bones and moves it up and down his stiff arm and leg, prodding the skin gently. The bone is in one hand as she manipulates the quill with the other, her bangles jangling, a look of deep concentration on her face.

She scarcely speaks during the treatment but the expression on her face grows graver. After sprinkling a fine white powder on to a tissue and telling the surgeon to inhale it, she wipes the muti from his body, packs her things in her bag and tells him: 'I will have to see you again, many times, but you will be OK.' He smiles and replies, 'Thanks for coming.' Later, he tells a visiting friend that he found her methods 'rather superficial', but adds: 'It can't do any harm and, who knows, maybe she's got something we don't know about.'

After the consultation, the surgeon's wife notices that Sara Mashele is walking very slowly and speaking in a slurred voice. 'You seem exhausted,' she comments. Sara replies: 'There are too many evil spirits in your husband. I have to take them out: they come from his body into me. Now I must go and wash myself with muti. When I come again, I will take some more bad spirits away from him, until he is well.'

The fee for the treatment is R500, payable after the first consultation. There is no further charge for her ongoing weekly visits, Sara tells the surgeon's wife. 'But at the end, when he is better, I will tell you how much you owe me.'

* * *

Sitting on the floor against the walls of a bare room in a Soweto house are fourteen people, who fall silent when a young woman enters. Dressed in white with white and ochre markings on her face, she holds a collection of animal tails bound together in a beaded handle. Her expression is preoccupied, almost crazed, her eyes wide and staring beneath a crop of tangled hair.

She starts to clap and they follow her time, repeating after her, over and over in loud voices, 'Inchanti', the Zulu name of a river snake. She raises her bare feet in rhythm with the clapping, lowers lightly to her toes, and stamps her heels. Wooden anklets rattle. The muscles of her body quiver, even on her cheeks, then tense as she stretches her arms. The dance speeds up, faster and faster; her feet spring high into the air, heels thumping in time with the clapping and the hysterical cry, 'Inchanti, Inchanti'. Stopping suddenly, she waits in utter stillness. The clapping and chanting cease and she falls to the floor, body heaving, face feverish. The room is silent until she rises and begins to speak in a frail tone, telling the audience about her dreams. Sobbing and trembling, they ask questions, exhorting her to confess what she has seen. Each time she speaks, they chorus 'Camagu', meaning 'Let the light shine'.

The performer, a trainee sangoma, is engaged in a ritual designed to achieve an altered state of consciousness. The rhythm of the chanting and dancing inspire transcendence: when she collapses, she is in a trance, the spirits having manifested themselves. While in this condition, the novitiate is a medium, speaking for the spirits. When fully trained, she will not need to dance in order to achieve supernatural communication. Experienced sangomas have only to call their ancestral song to mind when they require spirit possession. But the trainee, despite advanced suggestibility, is still acquiring the necessary mind control.

Her training may take up to ten years, especially if she has resisted her initial calling by the ancestral spirits. This comes in the form of a dream, always involving a snake. Variations of the dream persist and contain instructions on the type of clothing to be worn and the length to which her hair must grow. She frequently becomes ill, for no apparent reason, until she reveals her dreams. Then her elders know what has to happen: she must be sent to live with an eminent sangoma for the duration of her training. If she resists, having other hopes for her life, she will develop endless complaints, including paralysis of some of her limbs or mental illness. Sooner or later, as the dreams become ever more insistent, she will relent, if only to preserve her sanity.

While qualifying as diviners, many trainees learn the basics of herbalism from their mentors. It is a skill they then hone throughout their lives, by experimenting with plants and animal parts to achieve muti recipes they sometimes claim to have been given in dreams. Often there is an empirical rather than a mystical basis to these cures.

Being a Christian does not conflict with the call to traditional priesthood. Large numbers of Africans have been Christianised for four generations but have maintained a compound rather than a single belief. Over two thousand offshoots from orthodox Christian churches exist in Soweto today as sects combining Christian and indigenous religions. Although Christianity struggles to accommodate some of the exotic African forms, it is understandable that black Christians still fear the malevolence of witchcraft, just as surely as Europeans did at the time of the Renaissance.

Most black people believe in an almighty God who is so omnipotent that He is considered too lofty to attend to the pangs of individual human hearts and therefore surpasses mortal understanding. Dead ancestors, being spirits, can more readily communicate with God, mediating between Him and man. Sangomas — the prophets, physicians, psychiatrists and exorcists of African culture — are people chosen by the ancestors to interpret God's will on earth.

Sangomas fulfil a threefold function: religion, magic and medicine. They keep in touch with the ancestors to ascertain the cause of misfortune and its remedies; they expose evil-doers and identify witches, providing charms and muti with mystical properties to ward off evil; and, through the study of plants, they administer herbal extracts in the treatment of disease. The person requiring the sangoma's service goes to the diviner, who throws magic bones in order to discover the cause of the complaint, and then to the herbalist for treatment. Many sangomas combine both functions.

An estimated five thousand sangomas earn a living by practising their ancient profession in Soweto. Eighty-five per cent of all urban blacks regularly consult traditional practitioners, according to a survey conducted by the National Institute of Personnel Research. Most patients at Baragwanath

Hospital bear evidence of traditional healing: skin scarifications into which mutis have been rubbed, or charms and talismans worn on the body.

Although sangomas increasingly refer their clients to hospitals and clinics when traditional healing methods prove futile, patients sometimes resist hospitalisation. This is because witches are said to use bodily exuviae, such as nail and hair clippings, urine or stools, to harm their victims. People who believe in witchcraft fear their excreta might get into dangerous hands while they are in hospital.

Investigations into ritual murders have often uncovered sangomas, or witches, who use human body parts to make muti. The genitals of babies are particularly sought after; reports of infants mutilated for this purpose are not uncommon in Soweto. Some years ago, the murder of a ward cleaner at a white clinic in Johannesburg led to an alarming discovery. The cleaner had been killed because he was planning to report the incinerator stoker for selling human remains, swept from the operating theatre floor, to sangomas who believed they could make powerful muti from the limbs and internal tissue of living white people.

Modern doctors who decry sangomas most vociferously are the ones who know that critically ill patients could have been saved had they not wasted valuable time consulting traditional healers. Doctors treating a common form of septicaemia, the result of enemas made from crushed beetles, accuse sangomas of criminal activity because the highly acidic insects burn the lining of the intestine, often causing death.

Not surprisingly, Western medicine has maintained a sceptical distance from traditional healers, although doctors at Baragwanath admit to summoning sangomas in cases where patients can be helped psychologically through ancestor worship. 'The sangoma's special attire, his incantations, his amulets, charms and horns, portraying a man of great knowledge and mystery with an infinite number of secrets, handed down from his ancestors, give him an immense advantage over the rather ordinary looking Western doctor,' writes Michael Gelfand, a medical doctor and anthropologist. 'Thus in psychological therapy he is far superior to the scientific doctor who, unfortunately, tends to show little interest in the patient's family and background and so loses the confidence he could easily gain by a more friendly contact with his patients.'

Some doctors at Baragwanath — aware that the practice of psychiatry has only become a recognised science this century, and aware of international research showing that 40 per cent of illnesses originate in psychological disorders — realise they can learn from a local healing tradition which has prevailed for thousands of years.

There is much that South African medicine can learn from sangomas about the mentality of black patients. Just as every Westerner knows that we are continually exposed to germs, so do most Africans believe they are constantly threatened by the evil forces of witchcraft. The concept of chance has very little influence on the day-to-day philosophy of the average Sowetan. If he suffers serious illness or misfortune, he immediately looks for an explanation. Untimely deaths and accidents are particularly strong portents of evil. Someone, perhaps guided by an angry ancestor spirit, must have caused the misfortune. But who, how, and why? Only sangomas can provide acceptable answers, oust the evil, and offer preventative measures to ensure the trouble does not recur.

Western civilisation, being technology and concept orientated, relies largely on logical explanations while Africans live closer to the world of the unconscious and rely on their intuition and feelings; on images or dreams rather than concepts. Chance, an abstract idea based on the acceptance of chaotic happenings, can have no place in a worldview founded on belief in the unity and order of human experience. A scientifically explicable though unusual occurrence like the birth of twins, for example, is viewed with dismay in traditional African culture: a witch must have cursed the mother.

Apart from its effects on the practice of medicine, belief in witchcraft undoubtedly exerts a unique influence on society. It promotes polite behaviour, serving as a warning against hostile words and deeds; people are constantly reminded not to offend others because they might turn out to be witches. Since enmity is an expression of witchcraft, it should not be voiced openly for fear of accusations of sorcery. A sort of negative morality results: it is better not to make enemies because hatred is the mainspring of witchcraft.

In addition, the people accused of witchcraft conform to certain personality types, the characteristics of which are actively discouraged by society in order to avoid the evil label. The witch has an unhappy disposition, wears a sullen expression and rarely laughs. A person who is quiet and reserved or selfish and miserly runs the risk of being linked to witchcraft. But, at the other extreme, the person who achieves obvious wealth and success or is devoted to the pleasures of life is equally liable to be associated with evil. Children in traditional society — taught for generations to be pleasant and unassuming and to resist the desire to stand out from the crowd — have tended to adopt uniformly modest behaviour.

Dr Michael Gelfand explains: 'When examining the factors most important in causing the lack of material progress in Africa, one is forced to reconsider the importance of belief in witchcraft and ancestral worship for it seems that these beliefs are so intimately woven into everyday thinking that an exceptional attitude to conformity and change is created.

'Witchcraft is a theory of causation and, as a system of moral philosophy, has tremendous influence on behaviour because it is believed to be brought into operation by the witch when motivated by hatred, envy or greed. The more you have, the more likely you are to attract a witch's envy. Whether this attitude has militated against material progress in Africa is a subject for conjecture, but if belief in witchcraft has promoted mediocrity and dampened the individual's desire for material development, it must have impeded motivation.'

* * *

The witch's most fearsome power in African minds is her ability to 'eat' the immortal soul. A particularly tormenting feature of the belief is that witches tend to harm the people with whom they ought to co-operate: neighbours, friends or relatives. In a reversal of moral order, witches mock the decencies of society, becoming agents of destruction against kith and kin. As they invert morality, so they are seen in terms of inversion: they ride backwards on baboons, approach the homes of their victims backwards, work at night when normal people are asleep, go around naked, kill babies, eat human flesh, and consort with animals.

The malevolence of witchcraft lies in the belief rather than any real power. Common to many cultures worldwide prior to the spread of modern medical and scientific knowledge (the last English witch was burnt in 1722), it is a belief which helps to explain misfortune and provides society with scapegoats.

Reactions against perceived witchcraft are often brutal. For example, several men were sheltering from a storm on one occasion in Soweto when lightning struck the tree under which they were standing. One of them died. Hurrying by at the time was a luckless man on his way to work. Thought to have caused the accident and therefore to be a witch, he was caught and beaten to death. Another hapless victim of the witchcraft belief was a man who was running home naked, having been robbed by tsotsis of his new suit and underwear. Suddenly chased by an angry crowd, he was beaten to death with sticks. 'We thought he was a witch who had fallen off his baboon,' the murder trial later revealed.

More fortunate suspected witches are sometimes given the opportunity to repent. Their confessions, made through sangomas to the ancestral spirits, are witnessed by the people who believe they have been bewitched. In some ceremonies, when the witch beseeches the spirits to accept her confession, the sangoma takes a white chicken, slits its throat, and throws the bird into the centre of the gathering. Fluttering and jerking, the fowl is studied in its death throes to establish if it dies on its back with its feet in the air, signalling a cure. If it lies in any other position, the witch's confession is deemed incomplete. As many as a dozen chickens might be sacrificed before one of them dies in the correct position.

Witches are believed to inherit their supernatural powers. In some parts of South Africa, the witch parent is said to throw each new-born baby against the wall of the hut to test if it has inherited the role. Infants that cling to the wall like bats are the ones who will be carefully nurtured in the skills of witchcraft, beginning with charmed milk suckled from the mother's breast.

'Witches have superhuman qualities,' says anthropologist David Hammond-Tooke. 'They can fly through the air in a flash of time, can enter a house through a crack in the door, and can plunge their victims into so deep a sleep that they can be sent out wandering into the night, perhaps to secret rendezvous out in the bush where they are made to dance, egged on by beatings, so that their bodies are bruised and swollen in the morning when they wake. Xhosa witches in the Ciskei are believed to fly through the air by means of a flying machine made from the ribcage of a dead man... Witches are gregarious and seek each other out, often meeting naked at special places in the veld or bush...'

Witches usually assign familiars to conduct their evil deeds. These agents are either animals — the 'lightning' bird, owl, snake or wildcat, which are kept by witches as pets — or a well-documented monster, the thokoloshe, who features prominently even in Afrikaans mythology.

Descriptions of the thokoloshe vary but he exists, in one guise or another, in the minds of the majority of black people throughout Africa. He is a little man, never taller than one metre, with whom it is impossible to make eye contact. He has only one buttock and an extraordinarily long penis, which he slings over his shoulder. Some people believe he comes from the womb of the witch as a result of her copulation with a baboon; some think he is conjured up by witchcraft, or caught by sorcerers who lie in wait for him at night, keeping him a prisoner until he is indoctrinated as a familiar. The witch is said to use the thokoloshe as a sexual partner while he is undergoing training or when he is not representing her in the homes of her victims.

Some say he lives with the spirits under water. One of his favoured sports is seducing girls who come unsuspectingly to his pool to bathe or wash their clothes. It is extremely unwise to have an affair with a thokoloshe, though he is a masterly lover, because you may have a deformed child by him. A deformed baby is said to be proof of sex with a thokoloshe. Frigidity in a woman is sometimes claimed as the work of a thokoloshe lover.

Many Sowetan homes contain beds hoisted high on bricks as a defence against the thokoloshe's amorous advances. Another precaution, for decades a mystery to white employers whose domestic servants implore them to bring bottles of water back from coastal holidays, is to sprinkle sea water around the house in the belief that the thokoloshe smells the salt and is fooled into thinking he will have to cross an ocean in order to invade the house.

Some people identify the thokoloshe as a miner digging in his spare time for gold and diamonds, rather like the dwarfs in *Snow White*. 'He is not good or bad,' says one sangoma. 'He cannot do anything except what men tell him. Men are wicked, so he is wicked, but children can play with him and he is good to them.'

Says author Alistair Scobie: 'Where he appears, the thokoloshe is the source of all poltergeist phenomena, knocking, rapping, throwing things. Going bump in the night generally. Left to himself, the worst he will do is play pranks: curdle the milk or drink the beer left to cool. He might make a cow bear a stillborn calf, if you upset him, and he steals food. He may trip up one of the elders on the way home from a beer drink or scare the wits out of a bumptious young man... It is when a sorcerer captures him magically and trains him that he becomes willing to do all sorts of dirty work.'

Sangomas offer a variety of remedies as precautions against the thokoloshe. 'Wear snakeskin round the wrist,' says one. 'If you do not wish to look superstitious, get a snakeskin strap for your watch. A man should give him a bowl of blood. That satisfies him. For a woman it is perhaps best to let him sleep with her. But she must be careful, for he can steal her spirit.'

Sowetans of all ages believe in the thokoloshe. Twenty-three-year-old Thabiso Mono, once a fearless street warrior, is a political activist whose name appeared in newspapers throughout the world after he and the late Stompie Moeketsi Seipei were lashed by Winnie Mandela in one of the most infamous political assaults in South African history. A sophisticated young man today, Thabiso says of the thokoloshe: 'I believe in him because people, even my relatives, have told me stories which I believe are true stories. I have never had a thokoloshe on me but I would be frightened half to death if someone sent one to me. I hope it never happens.

'The thokoloshe makes you fight with people all the time. You cannot co-operate with anybody when the thokoloshe is with you, so you can't be happy with others. He tries to make you bad the whole time. If you have some money, the thokoloshe makes sure you waste it; he doesn't let you do anything important with that money.

'A witch can tell the thokoloshe to go to this woman and be her husband, make play with her, and then there is going to be friction between the husband and wife. The wife will sleep with the thokoloshe: she thinks it is her husband. The husband knows something is going on but nobody can see the thokoloshe. (It always has a small round stone in its hand, holding tight to it, and when it holds that stone it is invisible. The only way you can see the thokoloshe is if it drops the stone.) So the thokoloshe plays with the wife and wants the husband to get out of the house. The thokoloshe wants to be the man of the house now: that is what the witch told him.

'Nothing is normal in your life when the thokoloshe is with you. He can play silly tricks: switching off the kettle after you turned it on; taking food when you leave it on the plate. He can also do worse things, making abnormal things happen all the time, every day. At night, somebody told me, the thokoloshe switched on the hi-fi, very loud, and everyone in the house woke up. The man of the house went to switch it off. Then, even before he could go to sleep, the thokoloshe was playing like a baby with small cars, vroom, vroom, all the time, the whole night. Other nights, it sat on the window ledge, making noises like a cat, a dog or a wolf. That man could not sleep for a long time because of the thokoloshe.

'He had to go to a sangoma to take the thokoloshe away. My grandfather is a sangoma. He told me how the sangoma does this: he makes a bath with strong muti from the fields. He washes the person who had the thokoloshe sent to him, washes him very well, and then he pours the water from the bath far, far away from the house that the thokoloshe came into. When the sangoma is taking the water away, with the thokoloshe inside it, the thokoloshe will say: "Hai! Handifuni wena. Difuna lo bedithumelwe. Ku ye!" ("I don't want you. I want the person I was sent to.") But that person is clean now because of the muti which the sangoma put in the washing water. The thokoloshe can't go back to him: it has lost its power and can only go back to the witch. Or die.'

9

The Money Game

━━━▼▼▼━━━

When Sowetans throw parties, they mean business. Starting on Friday night and known as stokvels, they go on through Saturday, Sunday and often Monday. Guests pay dearly for the entertainment, emerging after three wild days with what they call TB — terrible bhabhalazi (hangovers) — and empty pockets.

They are parties with an earnest purpose: to raise money. An estimated R200-million is generated by stokvels in South Africa's black townships every month. Dating back a century and forming the basis of urban Africans' social life, stokvels are the means by which economically powerless people raise capital.

Very few Sowetans have the collateral to raise bank loans. If they want to open a backyard spaza, buy a taxi, give a child a university education or simply supplement the family's income, it is the stokvel that yields the money.

'A stokvel is a type of credit union in which a group of people enter into an agreement to contribute a fixed amount of money to a common pool weekly, fortnightly or monthly,' says Sowetan Andrew Lukhele, founder of the National Stokvels Association of South Africa. 'Then, depending on the rules governing a particular stokvel, this money or a portion of it may be drawn by members either in rotation or in a time of need. This mutual financial assistance is the main purpose of stokvels, but they also have valuable social and entertainment functions.

'Membership in a stokvel is voluntary. The introduction of a new member is made on personal recommendation. Honesty and reliability are important requirements for membership, as most stokvels do not have written agreements. This is one of the reasons why stokvels are often formed by neighbours, by people working at the same place, by members of the same family, or by members of a church congregation.'

Stokvels — with names like Tuesday Blues, Benneton, Shisa (hot), One Day Makes No Harm, and Malamogodu (entrails) — have between eight and twenty members, each of whom organises a party at least twice a year. The host receives 'table' money from every member, with which to buy food and drink. All must attend every party and a tally is kept of what they spend. It is incumbent on every member to match or exceed the amount spent by the others at his/her own party.

'The element of reciprocity is important at these stokvel parties,' says Andrew Lukhele. 'A member of a stokvel who supports the parties of another stokvel stands a greater chance of support when he hosts his own party than one who attends only the compulsory meetings of his own group. For this reason the host, with the assistance of the other members of his stokvel, does a subtle check to see who supported him and who did not.

'Similarly, lack of support for other stokvels can result in the decline of the standard of that stokvel. The more outgoing the members of a particular stokvel are, the more popular and powerful it becomes. Thus most stokvels apply certain controls to ensure that their members support other stokvels regularly.'

* * *

It is Sunday afternoon. We are driving around Rockville in Soweto — a place with a formidable reputation for drunkenness — looking for a stokvel party at 2344 Sotho Section. The people we ask for directions speak Afrikaans because they were 'removed' to Soweto from Western Native Township, a bulldozed settlement on the outskirts of Johannesburg which was tightly controlled by bureaucrats in their xenophobic heyday.

The house is next door to the police station, a reassuring feature which stokvel host Sfiso Sibanda has stated prominently on two hundred invitation cards handed to selected Sowetans during preceding weeks. We are early. Sfiso's wife Pinkie is ironing their party clothes. A chicken dish simmers in a giant pot in the kitchen, where Sfiso is packing an outsized municipal garbage bin with beers and blocks of ice.

The lounge, its regular furniture piled in the bedroom, is lined with functional hired chairs. An expensive sound system is on a cabinet, linked to a pair of enormous speakers which occupy much of the veranda. Sfiso's stokvel, called Doofis Jam IV, is serious about music. 'We go for jazz,' he says, 'but also disco. Come back later when the party is alive.'

We search Diepkloof for a second stokvel venue at 6563 Zone 4, driving up and down long narrow roads running parallel to a low-slung gold mine dump that blocks the skyline of Johannesburg from Soweto. In the last street, separated from the highway running alongside the mine dump by a narrow stretch of swampland, we see people suddenly surging out of their houses into the road, all looking towards the highway.

YOU ARE INVITED TO THE
"DOOFIS JAM IV"
Jammer: SFISO
– Venue –
2344 ROCKVILLE SOTHO SECTION
(NEXT TO THE POLICE STATION)
– Date –
11th & 12th DECEMBER '93
FOOD & DRINKS WILL BE SOLD
PEACE

Last guests linger at the end of a three-day Soweto stokvel party.
Photograph: Victor Matom

A vehicle of the kind used as taxis in Soweto is parked at the side of the highway, with passengers sitting inside. A man is dragging a small person from the vehicle — a child, no, a woman. He is punching her, drawing his fist far back for maximum force, in her face, her stomach. She falls, screaming. The crash barrier on the edge of the highway conceals her body from the street where the onlookers watch, aghast but unmoved to help the victim. It would take five minutes to run across the vlei, duck under the crash barrier, and overpower the bully. There are dozens of men watching but no one runs to her rescue. 'He has probably got a gun,' says one man. 'That's why he's doing it so openly. She can scream until she's dead; nobody will stop him.'

It is a sobering image to take to a party, which we find in the adjacent street. 'Welcome to Club Elegant and Cash Money Brothers' says a banner stretched across the entrance. The two stokvels operate together on money-making ventures.

It is the home of Revelation Xaba and his sister Phindile. He is unemployed and she is studying drama at the University of the Witwatersrand. They have three siblings, who are busy preparing for the party. Their parents have gone out for the evening.

Music blares. Streamers trail from rafters on the roof and from a wire fence enclosing the small garden. Eight Club Elegant women, immaculately groomed in orange and green linen, are blowing up balloons.

We go inside for a meal: T-bone steaks, pap and salads. Club Elegant's glamorous treasurer, wearing a straw hat decorated with white lace and an orange rose, hovers around the table keeping score of what we eat and drink. You pay for absolutely everything at a stokvel party: a handful of peanuts, a spoonful of gravy, a slice of bread are all extras. The prices are high by Soweto standards but everybody understands the logic. It is primarily a business venture.

Revelation hopes to 'double up'. He got R1 500 in table money from stokvel members and reckons he'll end up with R3 000 in his pocket. 'We will decide as a family what to do with the money,' he says. 'Some will go to pay Phindile's university, some for school fees for the younger ones. Some maybe to do something for the house.

'Some of the other Cash Money Brothers have used their money to open up a small business, as a hawker in town, or with a spaza shop in Soweto. You use the stokvel money to buy stock. One of the guys bought bricks to build a room behind the house of his parents for himself because there are too many in the house. Most of us are fund-raising for our families because we only have responsible guys in Cash Money Brothers.

'It's right that we use the money from the party for the family because they are all helping to make it a success. You use only your family because they are the only ones you can trust when there's money. I will buy new clothes for all of them from the money, to say thank you.'

Clothing is very important in Soweto. We sit in late afternoon sunshine on the lawn watching neatly brushed, stylishly dressed guests stream in from the street. Lovers who arrive hand-in-hand are sartorially blended; she in white pants and a patterned turquoise silk Hermes reproduction, he in white trousers and a shirt of many, matching colours. It is the current fashion: you can immediately see who belongs to whom by colour coding.

The volume of Revelation's 'high energy international disco' has soared. A child in the yard next door skips to the beat. People in the street are jiving. A supermarket trolley is wheeled in by two teenagers, who load it with empty bottles which they will exchange for fresh stock at Zak-Zak's — a nearby shebeen. Balloons are bursting; women shrieking. A Club Elegant girl has stitched so many beads in a dazzling design on her orange shorts that she cannot sit in them. 'I don't mind standing,' she says. 'It's even more important to look good than to be comfortable.'

When we leave, Revelation insists on escorting us to the car. He lingers, prolonging the conversation, looking over our shoulders at people in the street as he speaks. 'It is very good for me to have whites at my stokvel,' he confesses finally. 'That's why so many people are coming in.'

10

Maids & Madams

'It started on the night of the master's promotion party. The people from his work were coming to celebrate because he was made a director. We were cleaning the house, up and down, for the whole week. Somebody from the family brought old silver things, for candles and vegetables, and I polished them.

'On Friday night I was still there at 10 p.m. because the madam went to bed. She had a bad headache. I heard her vomiting about eight o'clock and then she called me to clean up. I was there already, by the door with the bucket. It happened before. I brought her a glass of water with ice, and she told me not to go off. I must wait for the master, to give him dinner.

'He came, after drinking. I took the dinner to him on a tray by the TV. I said, "Good evening, master", and he waved his hand, smiling. I was going out to my room but I heard some sounds so I went back. I passed the TV room. The tray was on the floor and the dogs were starting to eat the dinner. The master was shouting in the bedroom. I picked the tray up and went back to the kitchen. I got another plate and put the food nicely there and in the warming drawer because the dogs were making a mess.

'I heard the door of the bedroom opened. The master was shouting, "You can't be sick now!" He slammed the door. I hear him go to the TV room and I hurry up to get the dinner out. He shouted to me, "Violet!", so loud. I said, "Coming, master" in the squeaking voice that makes them laugh sometimes. I give him the tray. He says to me, "I hope everything is OK for the party." I said, "It's OK, everything is OK, master. Don't worry."

'Then I hear vomiting again. I go with the bucket. The madam is crying. I help her get back in the bed, take the face cloth to clean her, give some ice water. The master comes to the door. He shouted, "Violet, go off. The madam can clean her own face. It's late. Go off." I say to him, "She is sick, master. She must go to the doctor." Then he is very, very cross. He picked up the chair and threw it. The madam went under the bed. I ran out.

'On Saturday I come later to the house, seven o'clock instead of six. But this time, because of the party, the madam banged on my door, even before six. She was in her dressing gown. "Get up, Violet. We have a lot to do." I go to the kitchen. I start to make breakfast because the master and the kids are already in the TV room. The madam said, "We want breakfast early today, chop, chop."

'I take it. The master told Jeremy and Jackie to fetch their own trays from the kitchen because Violet is busy today. The madam was sitting there but she is sick, I can see. I give her the tray and ask her how she is. She said, "Fine, fine." But she did not eat. She is wearing her sunglasses with her dressing gown because the children must not see she was crying all night. It happened before.

'The master went in the car to the bottle store and the madam came in the kitchen. She is crying again. She told me, "Violet, what can I do?" She tells me all the things the master was doing to her. I just listened, shaking my head. We heard a car coming and she ran to her room to get dressed. It wasn't the master. It was her friend, bringing flowers for the rooms.

'The madam came out. "Make some tea, Violet," she told me. She was looking in the cupboard for vases to put the flowers in. She gives to her friend by the sink. There is one she can't find. "Where is the tall crystal vase, Violet?"

'I don't know what's crystal. I didn't see it. I looked but I can't find it. Her friend looked. Nothing. She's starting to get cross. "How many times have I told you to tell me if you break something?" she said to me. I told her I didn't break it. I was thinking maybe she lent it to one of her friends when they had a party, because they borrow from each other to make their houses look pretty. But now she is very cross. "That vase used to belong to my mother. I remember it when I was a young girl." She is shouting, pulling her hair. Her friend told her to calm down; there are enough vases.

'The master came back from the bottle store. Moses put the beers and bottles in the kitchen. The master sees his wife's friend, Evie, there so he is in a good mood. He put his arm round the madam. "Make some tea, Violet," he told me in a nice voice. I start again with the tea. Then I go to clean the house, make the beds. The madam's room is a big mess, everything lying around everywhere. Jackie is sitting by the dressing table making curls in her hair. I said to her, "Jackie, I must clean up", and she said, "Go ahead. I'm not stopping you." She is always cheeky to me.

'We worked hard, no stopping for lunch. I put the lunch in the dining room for the family at one o'clock and the madam said, "You can have a tin of sardines in the kitchen today, Violet, because there is too much to do." I don't want sardines so I had nothing. Moses also had nothing. He was cross and told me he wants to leave but I said, "Don't worry. These people pay good wages. You must stay or you will not find another good job like this." He went back to his work. He is young, Moses, and he told me once he would like to hit the madam when she is shouting at him in the garden. I am like a mother to him. I warn him what he shouldn't do. And he listened to me.

'At six p.m. everything is ready. The caterers were coming with the food. I asked the madam if I can go to my room to wash and put on my clean uniform. She told me to hurry up. All day she was lying down when the master was not looking. I can see she is still sick. But she is always sick, for a long time.

'When I was back in the kitchen, I cleaned up there. The madam and the master were in the bedroom. I looked around the house. It was beautiful; everything in place. I polished the silver again. The flowers are beautiful. There's some red candles in the silver things I polished; the glasses in lines on the table by the bar. The caterers brought a barman, a happy boy. He is very smart in a black suit with a bow-tie. He said to me, "Yes, mama, we will have some fun tonight." I started to feel happy myself.

'The madam and the master came from the bedroom. They were looking beautiful. The master is dressed the same as the barman, very smart. The madam put her hair up on her head, with a brooch on it. The dress she bought is very, very pretty; green with some beads on the front. She said to me, "Violet, how do I look?" I said, "Beautiful, I never saw you looking beautiful like this before." She laughed and holds my hand. But I can see she is sick, beautiful but sick. I know that woman.

'My job was to keep the kitchen tidy, take the plates after the guests have eaten and clean them, and wash glasses and bring them back clean. The master told me to come inside the party every half an hour only with the big tray to put glasses on. He doesn't want to see me in there all the time. I put the clock from the bedroom in the kitchen to check when it is half an hour. The lady from the caterers brought two waiters so I didn't have to serve that night. The kitchen was very much crowded with that lady and her waiters, and the barman coming in and out. I went to sit on the back step because there is nothing for me to do. The guests haven't eaten yet.

'I hear the master calling my name, "Violet, Violet: where is that bloody bitch?" I run inside. "I'm here, master." He's cross because somebody dropped a glass on the floor. "You must be here, ready when I want you," he said to me in a quiet voice, but very cross. "I told you I'll give you a big bonus tonight but only for working, not for loafing." I went in with the pan and the brush. The master was there with his arm round Evie. He said to me "Thank you, Violet" in a nice voice.

'Moses took beers that night and he was drunk. The master came and told me that I must stay in place of Moses until all the guests went home. The master was also drunk. I had to open the gate and close it for the cars.

'Very late in the night, when there was still drinking and dancing, I heard vomiting again. I listened at my madam's door, and got the bucket and went in. She was lying on the floor with a mess on her new dress, and blood also. I put her into the bed. She told me the master was having a nice party; leave him there. So I went back to the kitchen.

'After that party, my madam never came out of her bed. She went to hospital for some tests but they said they can't help her there. It was cancer. She must stay at home. Jeremy was very worried for her and he came to her every day from school, but Jackie stayed all the time with her friends. The master stayed drinking every night, same as before. When Jeremy was not there and I've finished the housework, I sat with her.

'We talked. I worked for her for thirteen years but we never talked like that. She talked to me, but I never talked to her. All things we said. She told me she was dying but I said, "You must hold on. Trust in the Lord." And we prayed.

'Near the end, she said to me, "Violet stay with me. Sleep on the carpet." The master was staying in the spare room. I think he was worried for her, but he wanted to run away, not stay with her. After that, I was there by her every night.

'One day she said to me, "Violet, I want to give you some things." I helped her out from the bed and she went to the cupboard. There's a safe in the back and she opened it. She gave me brooches, necklaces, earrings. I was afraid to take them but she said, "No, you must take. They came from my mother. You can sell them or keep, I don't mind." So I took them.

'After my madam died — she went to hospital for that — the master came to me, very cross. He said to me, " Where is the madam's jewellery?" I told him she gave it to me. I brought it from my room. He took it and phoned the police.

'They came and took me to the police station. They asked me questions: how long I been with that family, what my madam said when she was giving me the things. I told them. They let me go.

'I went back to the house and packed my things. I waited for the master to get my pay. He came again late, and drunk, with Evie. I said, "I am going. Please give me my money." He said to me, "No, Violet, stay. You are one of the family." I said, "No, I must go now." Then he got cross and said to me, "OK, go, bugger off." He took from me the key for my room so I couldn't get back inside. I was afraid, so I went. He never paid me.

'After, I heard from another girl that Evie went to live there with him. Maybe they got married.'

* * *

Painful testimonies of relationships between maids and madams are a feature of women's gossip in Soweto. Virtually every urbanised black woman in South Africa has been a domestic worker at some time in her life. Most of these relationships straddle the love/hate fault line so uneasily that they are forever joyless; at once intimate yet distant, caring yet callous.

Double standards abound, shifting like sands in the desert driven by the windy moods of the day. Though regarding her domestic worker as a potential thief from the moment she walks through the door, the employer nevertheless entrusts the care of her children to the maid's integrity. Though complaining constantly of the domestic worker's hygiene lapses, the employer continues to leave family cooking in the hands of her servant.

There are many and increasing exceptions, but dehumanising contradictions prevail. They have persisted for decades due to mutual dependency. The often ill-educated domestic worker has little choice but to find employment in the domestic sector. The employer, for all her complaints, is too accustomed to freedom from housework to go it alone.

Although liberating in itself, freedom from housework is not the employer's only gain from domestic labour. The services of a maid and gardener enhance the employer's ability to

Most employed black women work as servants in white households, taking care of their employer's children while neglecting their own.
Photograph: Louise Gubb

undertake work or business herself, so raising the household income. She also gains 'psychic income' — enhanced leisure — at low cost.

Some years ago, domestic workers got together to address the imbalance. Forming the South African Domestic Workers' Union (Sadwu), they aim to change the status quo in suburban kitchens. 'We are going to educate the madams,' says Margaret Nhlapho. 'We already have thousands of domestic workers negotiating with their employers. It's a pity there isn't a group who can represent employers. Then we could negotiate more effectively.'

The thrust of Sadwu's programme is publicising its minimum demands and teaching members to bargain with their employers. Violet Motlhasedi explains: 'Employers must wake up to the essential contribution domestic workers make to this country's economy. The economy would be seriously undermined if we suddenly withdrew our skills.'

Having established firm policies in respect of maximum working hours and leave, Sadwu finds the question of remuneration more problematic. Acknowledging that many whites cannot afford the minimum wage laid down by Sadwu, the union says poorer employers should pay for the time they can afford, thus freeing the worker to find part-time employment elsewhere. 'Sadwu will back up the demand with action,' says Violet Motlhasedi.

Dr Duncan Clarke, an economist who has studied domestic labour's prospects for reform, does not believe strike action is an option. 'Sadwu faces an atomised labour market, which is impossible to organise. The maximum number of employees will be 2−4 per household. So collective action is not feasible, especially in a labour surplus environment.'

The issue exciting whites to protest in the wake of Sadwu's demands is what they term the 'perks' of the live-in worker's remuneration — second-hand clothes, food rations and lodging, holidays with the family, 'leftovers' from the kitchen. That the acceptance of these unsolicited gifts in lieu of pay demeans the domestic worker, robbing her of the adult discretion to organise her life and spend her earnings as she pleases, is beyond the comprehension of many employers who continue to treat their servants as children.

In a study dedicated to 'the skeleton in the kitchen', Dr Clarke points out that non-cash benefits like rations and accommodation are often 30-50 per cent of gross value. However demeaning to the domestic worker, they cannot be written off by the employee. 'In respect of certain other items, such as foodstuffs which are regarded as "leftovers", the domestic worker gains a real benefit from additional consumption. This holds even though in functional terms the worker is in effect consuming the purchasing and consumption inefficiencies of the household,' he says. 'Leftovers', regarded as trash in many other societies, become employers' assets in South Africa. 'This is in direct contrast, though interestingly so, to the fictional character in N.F. Simpson's *One Way Pendulum*, a play in the theatre of the absurd, in which a woman is hired by a household to come in periodically and consume the "leftovers".'

There are around one million domestic workers in South Africa. Thirty per cent of Soweto households employ servants, who are often as exploited as those working in white homes. 'We want recognition that domestic workers are not super-human robots who don't mind working seven days a week, twelve hours or more a day for very little pay, away from their husbands and children,' says Violet Motlhasedi. 'Parents leave their most precious possessions — their children — in the hands of domestic workers, yet they won't pay them a living wage. They are extremely lucky that the workers take the job of caring for other people's children very seriously, while in many cases they have to neglect their own children.'

The effects of estrangement in their own families are heartfelt by domestic workers like Fikile Ngcobo: 'I know all the miseries of a domestic worker first hand. Their frustrations at living apart from their families and the problems they have at work and in the community form most of my childhood experiences. I was never emotionally attached to my mother because she was never at home with us.

'I would like to see a change of attitudes among domestic workers. I want them to be assertive and to know their rights as human beings and as workers. There should be a difference between the domestic worker of yesteryear and the present one.'

Margaret Nhlapho is among those at Sadwu who are teaching members to bargain for better conditions. 'Many of the white women who have now started to phone me to ask what we're doing are decent people who want to be fair. And many of the maids I talk to are fond of their madams, even in situations where they are exploited. What we have to do at Sadwu is encourage the maids to get rid of their inferiority complexes and stop being so frightened of losing their jobs that they allow themselves to be treated as doormats. I tell them, "You have to stand up for yourself, dears. If you don't, it's your own fault. If you don't want to call your employer madam, try calling her Mrs So-and-so one morning and see what happens. If she gets cross, say to her, 'We must talk'. Sit her down at the kitchen table and explain your position."

'I tell them that if they're having trouble with an old employer, try to get a job with a younger woman. The young whites are easier to teach. The older they are, the more they expect you to be a silent slave.

'I tell members about my own experiences as a maid. Wherever I worked I educated my madams. I tell them not to be afraid of the shouting and screaming. If they won't listen to you, then leave. Walk straight out the door. The madams will have to learn eventually because, when our membership spreads, they won't be able to find anyone who will put up with being a silent slave. Madams can't go on expecting maids never to answer back and defend themselves. It's completely unreasonable.

'I tell our members about the madam I worked for who used to get into bad moods and shout at me and criticise me for small things. One day her husband came in the kitchen and said, "Don't worry, Margaret, it's just that time of the month." I was cross and I told him, "Yes, I know. I'm also a woman. Do you think I don't have my periods too? Do you think I don't have bad moods too? But when I'm not feeling happy your wife makes jokes about my sour face. She expects me to smile all year round."

'Another time I had this madam who used to complain about the smell from my meat when it was cooking on her stove. One day she had some friends to tea and I deliberately put my meat on the stove without the lid, stirring it up, and making a very bad smell. She came in and said, "You know I don't like that smell in my house when I have guests." So I said, "Why don't you buy better quality meat so that it doesn't smell so bad?" Then she asked me to take it to my room and cook it there. But I said, "No, I'm not cooking in my bedroom. I'm cooking in the kitchen on the stove." She looked shocked and went back to her guests but the next day we sat down and talked and she realised she was being unreasonable.

'Then there was another madam who used to expect me to babysit every Wednesday when she played cards, and every Saturday when she went to the cinema. She never asked me. She just thought I knew her routine so that was OK. One Wednesday I put on my smart clothes under my overall and I washed up the dishes very quickly. I heard her calling, "Coooeee, Margaret, are you coming in?" I threw off my overall and went to the door where she could see me. "What are you doing in those clothes?" she asked me. "Don't you know by now that I always need you to babysit on Wednesdays?" And I said to her, "Yes, I know that, but don't you know that this is my time off? Don't you realise that I have a life of my own and I might want to do something on Wednesday and Saturday evenings? Why don't you ask me if it's convenient for me to babysit?" '

* * *

White South African women have come a long way on the rocky road to emancipation, to the point where that statement elicits no more than a wry or contemptuous smile. But the black South African woman: how far has she got in staking out the highroad for herself?

Not far, and in most cases, nowhere at all. Whereas the white woman is in the workplace in greater numbers than ever before, competing for responsibility, power and respect, the black woman finds little shift in attitudes — either from her own man, or the white men calling most of the employment shots in government, commerce and industry, or indeed from white women.

'Black women are the shock absorbers of the current political and economic crisis in three ways,' says sociologist Dr Jacklyn Cock. 'As workers, in the household, and as victims

179

of sexual and domestic violence. The black woman's power to endure, survive and create viable forms is a very moving story.'

Most employed black women work as domestic servants, a sector which is excluded from effective legislation affording protection against exploitation by employers. With profound implications for the welfare of the black urban family, many domestic workers are single parents, obliged to look after white children while neglecting their own. It is a situation that heaps shame on the concept of sisterhood among women at a time of reapportionment of opportunity, says Bernadette Mosala, a strident champion of black women's rights in South Africa. 'Consider the phenomenon of upper income women of all races realising their so-called liberation at the expense of the oppression and exploitation of lower class women.'

Although some domestic workers are cherished as surrogate mothers in white families, many more suffer lifelong assaults to their dignity. In *Working Women: A Portrait of South Africa's Black Working Women*, author Lesley Lawson interviews one domestic worker, identified as Stephanie, for whom the cruellest aspect of her job is not her employer's insistence on locking all the cupboards in the house while she is out at work; it is her habit of phoning home on occasions when she has forgotten to lock them and telling Stephanie to do so, then instructing her to call one of the children to hide the keys from the domestic worker.

A large proportion of the black women who are not employed in private households work as office cleaners. They scrub and dust at night, long after South Africa's cities have gone to sleep. Nomvula, another who tells her luckless tale in *Working Women*, says she lies on a bare office floor trying to rest for two dark hours after finishing her cleaning duties at 3.30 a.m. every weekday. She cannot go home at that hour since no transport runs to her township until 5.30. She arrives just in time to prepare breakfast for her children before they leave for school. Then she sleeps for three or four hours, rising to clean her own home, wash and iron her family's clothes and prepare the evening meal. By 2.00 p.m. she is back on the bus for the first leg of her journey to begin work four hours later.

'This job makes me sick,' says Nomvula, who has been doing night work for twenty years. 'You've got sore eyes and you've got headaches all the time because you don't sleep full hours.'

The gender gap in black society is closing so slowly that changes are barely perceptible. Few black husbands help their working wives with chores at home. 'My husband thinks if his friends find him sweeping they're going to say he's stupid,' complains Nomvula. 'So he can't do anything. He just sits there with the paper.'

'In the majority of black families, the husband is away from the home more often than he's in it, not only working but out socialising by himself,' says Suzette Mafuna, a public relations consultant. 'Often he'll spend nights away without letting her know, and she has no right to query this... She does everything but there's no doubt who's the boss: he is. If she tries to protest, she'll lose him to another woman.

'Often, because of shortages of accommodation, the family has to live with his parents — never her parents, because the wives traditionally belong to the husband's family. He is very protected there, and his wife dare not complain. The concept of women's liberation is laughable in the African context. It's far too advanced. Whereas the Jane Fondas are changing the world, we still have to sort out basic domestic issues, and most of us are a long way from making any progress at all on the home front.'

Musa Myeni, a politician, believes black women can expect nothing but trouble if they overstep domestic boundaries.

'Men like variety and if you stand in their way, you will get bruised. Men of all races find monogamy difficult, and black men find it almost impossible.

'Women are quick innovators but they're dealing with conservative men who want to feel that they're in charge. If a woman deprives him of this need, she'll destroy him. Powerful women in the Western sense don't find husbands in black society. Men avoid them, or divorce them. And divorce still carries a strong stigma in black society. The sensible black woman relies on tact rather than competitiveness to secure change.'

Journalist Pearl Luthuli's career victories, like the triumphs of virtually every commercially successful black woman in Soweto, are hard-won. 'Stereotyped roles have not changed much in black communities. Woman's place is in the kitchen. When a man talks, she must shut up. But men die, or they divorce us, and then we discover that we can think for ourselves.

'I got married at twenty-one and went straight from my father's authority into my husband's. I couldn't drive or even do the shopping by myself. When my husband, who was a musician, was out of town I did nothing with my own life; just waited for him to return. He died tragically in a car accident. I thought the world had come to an end, but I slowly discovered that I had brains of my own.

'Black women have a dual disadvantage in South African society: their gender and their colour. But women perpetuate their inferior status by making their sons feel superior. When we have a son, we teach him to be a man rather than a person, and we teach our daughters to be subservient. So many black women are moaning about their husbands' attitudes while raising their sons and daughters in exactly the same image.'

11

Died in Soweto

T he funeral service for Busisiwe Lilian Matsimbi, born in
Soweto in 1944, is held at her home in Phiri. A wizened,
bearded priest wearing the blue and white cassock of the Zion
Christian Church conducts the solemn proceedings in a striped
red tent pitched outside the house. Women relatives of the
deceased squat on the ground beside the coffin, shrouded in
blankets despite intense heat, while the men in the immediate
family sit on chairs with the priest. The rest of the congregation stands shoulder to shoulder in the tent and beyond its
hoisted entrance, down the side of the house and in the street.

The priest leads the service in prayer. The mourners
harmonise 'Amen' and begin a soft, sad hymn. The women
huddled together beside the coffin weep soundlessly and sway
in unison. As the priest fumbles through his Bible, the mourners
hum, some in descant, their sweetly muted voices rising in
waves of sorrow.

Embarking on a passionate sermon, the priest shouts and
gesticulates. Nobody in the congregation stirs in ten minutes of
rapt devotion. When he stops speaking, he points to the
entrance of the tent, beckoning for someone to enter. The

heads of the mourners turn to look at a lone white woman standing there. They call, 'Come in, come in,' until she realises they are summoning her, a stranger witnessing the rites of passage in Soweto. 'You are welcome,' says the priest. 'Would you like to speak?'

The congregation begins to sing in English, a haunting hymn often heard in Soweto:

Give your love to Africa, we are brothers all,
Who by sin and slavery, long were held in thrall;
Let the white man love the black and when time is passed,
In our Father's home above, all shall meet at last.

Two of Busisiwe Matsimbi's male relatives pay tribute to her. She worked hard all her life and bore her burdens with courage. She fought for justice and helped people whenever she could. She was calm and truthful; a good wife and mother. When one of the speakers falters, overcome with emotion, the mourners hum, giving him time to recover.

He recalls the day Busisiwe walked to Baragwanath Hospital to visit her dying mother and didn't come home for five days because she couldn't bear to leave the old woman alone. A doctor at the hospital gave her permission to sleep under the patient's bed until death came.

The other speaker, Busisiwe's son, tells a long story about a job he once took in Johannesburg, which required him to dress up in a Father Christmas suit and distribute leaflets door-to-door. As he walked along the streets day after day, whites in cars waved to him. Children ran up to greet him gleefully. When he discussed this puzzling warmth with his mother, she said it was because the suit and the white cotton wool beard covered up his black skin.

The massed voices soar as eight Peaceful Burial Society women — dressed in black and white, each carrying a lighted candle — file alongside the coffin. The priest chants praises, endorsed by bursts of wailing from faces cast heavenward. A member of the burial society reads the messages on wreaths of plastic flowers, holding her candle aloft in a steady hand despite the hot wax that spills down her arm.

Leading the funeral procession from the tent, the priest chants exuberantly. As he steps into the sunshine, a low roll of drums sounds and drum majorettes in starched yellow and white dresses high-step into the dirt road ahead of the hearse, where they stand to attention. The drums are still as the coffin is placed in a gleaming grey funeral coach belonging to Poonees, one of the most prestigious undertakers operating in Soweto. Caps Poonee and his brother Biekes, who are Indians, run a fleet of fifty funeral vehicles, which are sometimes hijacked in Soweto.

The chief mourner and her close kin ride in a matching grey Cadillac stretch limousine as the funeral cortège moves slowly forward, led by the prancing dancers and several young drummers beating time. The rest of the mourners are crammed into three large buses, hired from the municipality. This is an average funeral by Soweto standards: often six buses are required.

It is midday. The sun is high and hot. The pace of the drum majorettes quickens until they are running. A siren shrieks from the hearse to warn traffic in the main road ahead. Suddenly the dancers spring into the air, bouncing to the side of the road in perfect symmetry and a flare of yellow skirts.

The hearse speeds up, driven by Biekes Poonee. He has made the journey to Avalon Cemetery hundreds of times, often attending three or more funerals on a single Saturday. 'A

A typical Soweto funeral, held in a tent pitched outside the home of the deceased.
Photograph: Victor Matom

funeral is about the only event that takes place on time in Soweto, otherwise we wouldn't be able to bury everybody. Traditionally, funerals have to take place at certain times of the day.

'We do funerals in all of South Africa's communities. I can say that the blacks feel and express the sorrow of death much more than anybody else. They want a dignified funeral, and we were the first undertakers to respect their wishes in Soweto, over thirty years ago. Before we came with beautiful vehicles the dead went to their graves in carts and trucks.'

He recalls one of Soweto's many memorable funerals, twenty years ago, when Lilian Ngoyi — among the ANC's most revered activists — was buried at Avalon. 'I came with the funeral coach but they told me they didn't need it. They said they were bringing her on a cart. They packed the wreaths into the hearse and I drove behind the horse and cart. It was a massive funeral. The police came to interview me afterwards. They wanted to know the colour of the cloth covering her coffin.'

As we drive into Avalon, a vast graveyard, Biekes points to a distant part of the cemetery where Lilian Ngoyi is buried, beneath the body of her friend and fellow fighter for black liberation, Helen Joseph, one of the few whites laid to rest in Soweto.

The cemetery is a tangle of hectic activity and neglect. Its roads are shallow rivers of rain water, impassable without risk of sinking into mud. Dozens of buses, hearses and mourners' limousines weave their way across the waterlogged veld separating one stretch of graves from another. When we arrive at Busisiwe Matsimbi's final destination, Biekes inspects the mud-spattered hearse with dismay. 'This vehicle has to do other funerals today, and look at the state of it,' he complains.

'Once, all the buses and vehicles got stuck in the mud. We had to wait until Monday to tow them out. The mourners had to walk back to their homes. It's so disorganised. If all these mourners today don't remember the number of the bus they came in, they can get on the wrong one and finish up in some other part of Soweto, miles from home.'

Tall weeds obscure the older graves; tattered wreaths tumble about in the wind. The sickly-sweet smell of khaki weed fills the air. There are no trees. 'The only tap is far away over there,' says Biekes. 'Mourners often faint from grief and heat so we carry water with us.'

The hide of the cow which has been slaughtered to feed guests at the forthcoming funeral feast is laid over the coffin. Busisiwe Matsimbi is lowered into the earth. A concrete slab goes into the grave, a precaution against theft of the casket. The priest recites the last rites. The chief mourner screams and falls to the ground, a dark mud stain spreading on her blanket. She is helped to her feet but falls again. Mourners file slowly past the grave. Each has a handful of soil to spill over the coffin. 'Hamba kahle' ('Go well'), they say in quiet voices.

✳ ✳ ✳

Death has two vital qualities which must be reflected in African funeral rituals. Synonymous with entry into the spiritual world of the ancestors, it is a journey of utmost importance, requiring scrupulously observed rites. Secondly, because death is thought to contaminate living relatives, cleansing rituals form the basis of many funeral rites.

Although burial proceedings on the day of the funeral are similar to those practised throughout the Christian world, the corpse so pollutes its community through ritual impurity that certain taboos are imposed on the family, including in some cases a ban on sexual relations, or on the consumption of certain foods. The gravediggers of traditional society were required to perform their tasks naked so that their clothing was not contaminated. Widows in Soweto today must wear one set of garments throughout the twelve-month grieving period, which are burnt when the mourning term ends. All those attending funerals must observe a ritual cleansing procedure before partaking of the funeral feast.

Another precaution against ritual impurity is the inversion of behaviour and speech. Some, including traditional Nguni and Sotho, remove the corpse from the hut through a hole made at the back of the dwelling on the day of death, rather than through its entrance. Zulus enter the deceased's house in reverse so that their footprints go out rather than into the aura of death.

The proper burial posture of the corpse in traditional culture was a squatting position, with the knees up — which is also the birth position and symbolises entry into the spirit realm. If rigor mortis had set in before burial, the tendons at the knees and elbows were cut in order to bend the limbs. This was sometimes done regardless of stiffness so that witches could not steal the corpse and use it as a zombie familiar to conduct evil deeds. Further precautions against witchcraft included filling the grave with stones and inspecting it nightly for a period after burial.

The symbol Africans use to make contact with their ancestors is blood. All rites of passage — marking the deceased's separation through death, transition to the spirit world, and reincorporation as an ancestor among the living — begin with the sacrificial slaughter of an ox, goat or chicken.

The animal is killed with a sacrificial spear kept only for this purpose. Stabbed just below the sternum and into the thorax, it does not die immediately. Its desperate cries and convulsions find no response among the people present, who are in communion with their ancestors. Because ancestors are said to be pleased if the animal cries a lot, its agony is often deliberately prolonged. There is no notion of cruelty to the doomed creature. Its death is a necessary, ritual event. After a goat has died and been dismembered, it is sometimes thought auspicious to cause the beast to 'smile'. Its severed head is held up and the mouth slit along the jawline to the ears so that long rows of teeth are bared in a macabre grin.

The dead of yesteryear did not depart without their important possessions. Snuffboxes, spears, spoons, pipes and blankets were interred with the corpse. Whether these were thought to be needed in the next world or buried because of their ritual impurity is unclear. Food — including pumpkins, grain and other items containing seeds — was also placed in the traditional grave as an incentive for the deceased to ensure good crops for his living relatives.

A firm distinction was traditionally drawn between the rites accorded those who died of natural causes and those who perished through violence. Nguni who died violently were never buried in the kraal for fear it would be contaminated by their fate. A person struck by lightning was sometimes required to be buried near a river in moist soil because the accident had rendered the victim ritually hot and therefore a possible target for future lightning bolts. The corpse of a drowned man had to be buried beside the river in which he sank in the belief that its waters, if cheated, would claim other victims.

Some traditional burial procedures have been superseded by Christian rituals in Soweto, where an estimated 90 per cent of the community belong to Christian churches. But most of the old customs survive, some in modified forms. A new blanket invariably covers the corpse. Personal belongings often go inside the grave. Sophisticated blacks introduce modern offerings. One Sowetan priest reports that the daughter of a prominent businessman placed a set of expensive pens and a popular novel in her father's grave.

* * *

A widespread innovation which today plays a prominent role in township funerals is the burial society. It is an exclusively women's institution arising out of employed people's desire to ensure they be decently buried themselves, as well as in a financial position to afford proper burials for their close relatives. Families in Soweto that cannot afford to bury their dead are given pauper graves by the state, a humiliation they avoid at all costs.

Midwife Julie Manganyi is the chairwoman of Khomanani (Togetherness) Burial Society in Soweto. It consists of twenty-five members, most of whom have been friends since their schooldays. 'We pop out money to a member to pay for the funeral when somebody in her family dies,' explains Julie. 'And not only money for burial but also to buy cows, goats, vegetables and drinks. It's written in the constitution we all signed that we are there to help the bereaved family with money and with our hands.

'When we join, we must each declare the family members we choose for burial. When one dies, we scratch the name from the list. You have your immediate family — husband and children — plus four others, maybe parents or grandparents. When your mum dies you like to say thank-you by burying her in a nice casket, for what she has done for her kids. I have only myself, no husband, and one child, plus four others. There are some in Khomanani with more children than others so they get more money, but it doesn't matter.'

Though existing primarily as self-help support groups in times of death, burial societies also provide entertainment and function as savings schemes for their members. 'We have fun together when death is not around,' says Julie. 'And we can afford to buy things for ourselves and our homes that we couldn't save up for if we didn't have the society.

'Each member pays R230 every month. We have a meeting once a week, when one person is given R50 to spend on herself. Upon death, the member draws R1 500 to pay to the undertaker. Then we provide money for the beasts and the food. We go to the house of the member to comfort her family and cook for them throughout the whole week of the funeral preparations. On the day of the funeral we prepare and cook, everything, wash the dishes afterwards, everything.

'For fun, we have special things at Christmas and at Easter. We organise ourselves to go some place like a hotel for a party, to eat and drink. We have "Secret Pals" at Christmas. Everybody writes her name on a piece of paper and what she wants for a present: an electric frying pan, some floral sheets, anything she likes. They fold the papers and each draws one. Each gets R200 from the treasurer to buy the secret present written on the piece of paper. You don't know who is buying for you so it's fun at the party to find out. Then each member has also been given another R50 to buy a thank-you present for the one who bought her the big present. You collect so many nice things.

'But really we are there for the funerals. We believe you have to prepare the way for the ancestors. Everything must be right for them or they will bring you trouble. It is a very important matter for us blacks. Even when you do everything right, they still come to you. I have many dreams. Often I'm at a party but then it's a funeral, and my grandmother is there telling me to pray. I loved my grandmother a lot — we used to console ourselves with her — so she comes to me more than others, but there are others, even the ones I didn't know. They tell me things; don't do this and that, go there, stay here. If I'm doubtful about anything, I never do it because I think maybe one of my ancestors told me not to do it in a dream which I didn't remember in the morning.

'Sometimes I get tired of all these people telling me what to do. But when we need to consult them, it's good. They help you. We slaughter a goat, go to the cemetery early in the morning and invite the ancestors to come to the house to advise us.

'If you have an ancestor who was a happy person, and you have a baby who cries a lot, you can slaughter a white chicken, go to the graveyard and ask that happy ancestor if you can change the name of the baby to her name. Then the baby can be happy also. That's why we don't forget our ancestors. They can help you, or they can mess you up.'

* * *

Death is the greatest enigma of human experience. African culture comprehends it more successfully than Western societies because black people discovered long ago that they could 'tame' death by bringing the deceased back into the world of the living as ancestors.

Reincorporating the dead into the community is among the most important ceremonies performed in Soweto. A ritual conducted after the mourning period, it spans several days or weeks, depending on the traditions of various groups. It usually commences with a beer drink and involves the sacrifice of two or more beasts.

'Although black people go to a lot of trouble and expense to bury and mourn their dead, it's a contradiction,' says the

Reverend Otto Mbangula, a minister of the Methodist Church. 'They don't really believe you die. They believe you go to the bigger family of ancestors. They can call on the ancestors for guidance any time, just as the ancestors come to them in dreams all the time.

'If a man comes from the village to live in Johannesburg and doesn't get a job, he picks up a chicken, slaughters it and goes to the cemetery for advice. His belief is that the dead are alive, they remain, they understand.

'Death is perceived with awe and great respect, even though the people believe it's not actually death but part of a journey taking you to an honoured position where you continue to live in your family and community.

'When there's a death in Soweto, you'll see more than just sadness in the family. It will permeate throughout the larger family, the community, everyone who was connected to the deceased, including strangers living in the streets nearby. If my child dies, the pain is not only mine. It goes to all. That's why people travel so far, often at great expense, to attend a funeral.'

One of the few African traditions that has survived urbanisation intact is the mourning of the dead, says the Reverend Mbangula. 'Even though they're born in Soweto, the people are soaked in the traditions surrounding death. People must wear a symbol on the arm to let others know, "I am weeping". They can't visit at certain times. When the sun sets, they must be back inside the house. The chief mourner doesn't move out of the house. They must mourn. They can't take it lightly. It's a loss.'

Another Methodist minister, the Reverend Dan Twala, describes mourning rituals inside the home of the deceased. 'Immediately the death is known, the relatives must await the

The chief mourner, covered in a
blanket, guides a relative as he
shovels soil into a grave at Avalon
Cemetery in Soweto.
Photograph: Victor Matom

arrival of the head of the family. There must be one person, usually the chief mourner, sitting on a mattress in the room where the deceased slept. There must all the time be a lighted candle in the room to indicate that the light of this life is not gone. Photographs or pictures must be removed from the walls of the room. Nothing must divert attention from the death. Others come into the house and pray. Others bake and cook meals for the family. Others just sit, not saying anything. What they are saying without words is, "You are not alone: we are with you." The procession of people in and out intensifies as the days pass and the funeral comes nearer.'

Residents of Soweto attend funerals more frequently than any community in the world. They are continually aware that they might die at any moment because untimely death lurks on every street corner. Life is cheap. Soweto's traumatic history has destroyed much of the social fabric previously holding the community together. The black family, once an unassailable institution, is today frail and inadequate. Yet, just when you are ready to conclude that Soweto is in catastrophic decline, you find a breathtaking paradox. Funerals reveal that the family is unbroken, after all. The community does pull together. But its resilience, the life-affirming element, finds expression mainly at funerals — in death — rather than in day-to-day life.

'Death brings a most important thing, unity, to our people,' says the Reverend Twala. 'Nobody wouldn't come to the funeral because he's been in conflict with you. We come together as one at funerals, more than at weddings. People will travel from anywhere to mark death, but not marriage. Death is much more important.'

The Reverend Paul Verryn, one of a handful of whites living in Soweto, says funerals are a continual reminder to him of the quality of Soweto's community, despite much evidence to the contrary in everyday life. 'It comes down to the fact that they're committed and connected to each other, not in superficial, sentimental ways, but in a real solidarity. There is no death that cannot be contained by this community. No matter how dreadful the circumstances, the community will be there to carry you through the agony you've got to face. You'll never face it alone. I've very rarely come across a death that is not mourned fully. If you die and nobody comes to mourn you, you must know that the community considers you a very bad person indeed.

'Black people exercise an enormous amount of religious tolerance at funerals. Whatever best sends the deceased on the journey to the world of the ancestors is acceptable. They're bonded to the individual, rather than to the symbols of the church. When we bury a young criminal, it's razzmatazz stuff. The friends steal cars as a tribute to the deceased, which they wreck and burn inside the cemetery near the grave. They shoot guns in the air and into the coffin. There's a real defiance of religious form; a deep commitment to anarchy.

'But the community respects whatever has to be done for that dead person in order for the mourners to come to terms with what's happened in their lives. They don't complain about the way the criminals mourn their dead. The community says the people who are grieving have to choose the way they will grieve. Whatever makes the most sense and enables them to express with greatest integrity the love they have for the person who has passed on is the most important rite of passage the bereaved have to deal with at that time. It transcends age, culture and religious or political belief. They're not seeking salvation from sin; they're accepting death.

'There are times when these young criminals attend funerals without displaying their defiant behaviour. We had a young girl in our congregation who was disabled. She was a really nice person; everybody liked her. She was waiting for a taxi. Another taxi overtook a vehicle and swerved on to the pavement, collecting her. She was killed. Her funeral was held by youngsters, including criminals. They came from miles around to pay their last respects in the traditional manner. At the end of the day, you see tremendous cohesion in Soweto.'

Epilogue

I t is not easy to see — and still harder to achieve — progress in a place like Soweto. But it is there.

A fundamental feature of developing Africa is the migration from village to city of people wishing to escape rural limitations and become active and viable members of modern economic and social systems. The breakdown of ethnic origins therefore represents both the emancipation of individuals and the birth of a new society.

Exploiting the resources of South Africa has involved the concentration of labour and skills in the towns. The rural areas of the country may never produce adequate prosperity from the soil for rural-based Africans. Urbanisation, driven by a potentially incurable rural poverty, appears the only way forward.

Soweto's filthy streets and rickety shacks, representing a painful stage in a difficult transition, are not mere evidence of African decline. They are signs of escape from the hope-lessness of a collapsed ethnic system. South Africa's richest optimism is embedded in these overcrowded, unsightly, crime-ravaged, disease-ridden townships. They represent the black person's forced choice and willingness to undergo a punishing apprenticeship in pursuit of a new life. They reflect the positive statement of Sowetans' courage, tenacity and hopes.

Even the bleakest shanty town in Soweto is the site of learning. Its most malnourished, illiterate resident has discovered how to negotiate traffic, bank money, and adjust to the rigours of an alien discipline of structured and imposed punctuality. The sordidness of the Sowetan environment conceals many accumulated achievements, including a stake — however mean and disproportionate — in the wealth of South Africa.

Like the medieval peasants of Europe, who endured long generations of sickness and hunger in unfriendly cities, Sowetans are preparing for the day when their descendants become the new captains of industry, doctors, engineers, poets, artists and modern visionaries of every kind.

Life in Soweto may be squalid and tense, but it is also creative and exciting. The majority of Sowetans may be humble, yet they are undiminished. They have made meaning of burdensome daily struggles which are often quite wrongly perceived as pathetic by inexperienced observers.

The light of contemporary history shines in Soweto's homes and hearts beyond the inequities of apartheid to a new recognition of the realities of South Africa's future. The Soweto shack constructed from factory refuse, with a pot of vivid geraniums beside its sagging door, is the symbol of a proud people facing the coming millennium with boldness and enterprise. The deeply complex politics of South Africa, its desperate past and uncertain future, are giving way to new visions dreamed and realised inside the hovels of Soweto.